THE KNITTER'S CURIOSITY CABINET VOLUME II

HUNTER HAMMERSEN

THE KNITTER'S CURIOSITY CABINET VOLUME II

18 PATTERNS INSPIRED BY VINTAGE BUTTERFLY ILLUSTRATIONS

HUNTER HAMMERSEN

PANTSVILLE PRESS

Photography by Zoë Lonergan

Book design and cover design by Zoë Lonergan

Charts created with StitchMastery Knitting Chart Editor

ISBN: 978-0-9849982-2-7

First Printing, 2013
Printed in China with Asia Pacific Offset

Pantsville Press
Cleveland, Ohio
www.pantsvillepress.com

CONTENTS

INTRODUCTION

One isn't a collection. One thing by itself is just an object. One thing by itself might even be an accident. To be a proper collection, you need at least two (and I fear you may actually need three). Collecting and collections are at the very heart of *The Knitter's Curiosity Cabinet*, and I knew from the moment the idea for these books first came to me that I wanted there to be more than one.

I love curiosity cabinets, both the objects themselves and the spirit of exploration and discovery they embody. The idea of a knitter's curiosity cabinet (an assemblage of lace and cables and ribbings instead of the more traditional rocks and shells and leaves) has tremendous resonance for me.

For the first book, I found inspiration for the patterns in vintage botanical prints (these sorts of prints were one of the primary ways people documented and shared the contents of their own cabinets with the world). For this book, I wanted to continue with the same theme but also to work with some new material. When I came across collections of beautiful illustrations of butterflies, I knew they would work perfectly. Each print has again served as the starting point for both a sock and an accessory. And once again, I hope you'll find something here worthy of being added to your own collection of knitted treasures.

ACKNOWLEDGEMENTS

I've noticed an odd contrast in how I create these books. Parts of the process are deeply solitary (please don't talk to me while I'm doing math; it won't end well for either of us), but parts of it are wonderfully communal. With each new project, I come to rely upon, and appreciate, these communal aspects of the process more and more. I could never do this alone. Thanks to these marvelous people, I don't have to.

I'm lucky enough to have the help of an amazing group of test and sample knitters. These women work miracles. They get my patterns in the roughest imaginable form and somehow turn my jumbled instructions into beautiful things. Along the way, they help transform the patterns into something ever so much more presentable and easier for others to follow. They are Carol Baird, Christy Herbert, Barb Stephenson, Beth Loft, Antonia Markiet, Angela Grob, Lise Brackbill, Jessica Powers, Audrey Tam, Michele Marshall, Lila Guterman, Katie Metzroth, Sara Varty, and Ellen Stratton, and I am in their debt.

My editors are also both miracle workers. Cathy Scott is the genius responsible for StitchMastery, the software used to make the charts in the book. That alone would be enough to earn her my undying gratitude, but she's also the best tech editor I could ask for. Her clarity of thought and attention to detail are unparalleled. What Cathy does for my patterns, Heather Ordover does for my prose. She gently, tactfully (and without ever once sending me a sheet of paper drenched in great splashes of red ink) points out my crimes against the English language and makes sure I actually say what I mean.

While the editors and knitters were hard at work refining the text and charts, another talented group of people were busy making the book both lovely and easy to use. Stacy Siddle, Lauren Falk, and Laura Stockert were kind enough to squander a perfectly good Saturday flaunting knitwear in a host of unusual places and poses. They remained both gracious and poised in the face of a never-ending stream of requests to "scoot your toe over just a bit, turn your heel that way, lift that cuff ... ok, now, just relax and look natural." The enchanting Elle Gemma worked her magic and made everyone look radiant. James Edmonson, Jennifer Nieves, and Laura Travis of the Dittrick Medical History Center and Dzwinka Holian of the Allen Memorial Medical Library let me use their delightful facilities once more. The location is perfect, and I was thrilled to be allowed to invade it once again.

Behind the camera was the perpetually charming Zoë Lonergan. Zoë designed all the *Knitter's Curiosity Cabinet* books, and I'm delighted to have had her expert eye for the photography in this one too. She has a tremendous ability to take pictures that are both lovely and informative (you knitters know exactly what I mean; getting both in one shot is hard). I couldn't be more pleased with the photos or the layout.

Slightly removed from the daily workings of the book, but no less important, are Cat Bordhi and the members of her Visionary Authors program. This group provides a perfect blend of moral support, practical advice, and an occasional kick in the pants. It is a wonderful collection of people, and I'm lucky to be a part of it.

And of course, many thanks to my family. It would doubtless be easier for them to answer lawyer or engineer or professor when people ask just what it is I do, but they seem rather taken with this odd endeavor of mine and have been tremendously supportive of it. Finally (and always), uncountable thanks to my husband Brian. His abiding faith in me is the reason these books exist. I couldn't do it without him.

HISTORY

I have a confession to make. When I wrote the history section for the first volume in this series, I didn't think anyone would read it. I figured either people already knew everything they wanted to know about curiosity cabinets or they would be in a hurry to get to the patterns. Either way, my suspicion was that most people would skip right over that bit and dive straight into the rest of the book (though there was one rather rough night when I dreamt that all my former history professors not only read it but came to my house to chastise me for not including footnotes).

Much to my surprise, people actually seem to have read it. Not only that, people seem to have enjoyed it. Somet version of "oooh, tell me more about curiosity cabinets" is probably the most common request I get when I talk about the book. That is both very flattering (if I hadn't started writing knitting books, I was going to be a history professor. I have a tendency to launch into unprompted lectures if not carefully watched) and the tiniest bit nerve-wracking (me, you're asking me? But others are so much more qualified). It also makes it ever so much harder to write this section this time. Someone might read it; that makes it scarier. This is a huge subject (people spend their careers studying it), and I know I can't do it justice in a few pages. I've arrived at a bit of a compromise. I'll briefly (oh so very briefly) sketch the history of curiosity cabinets, then I'll tell you a bit about the development of collections with a specific focus, then I'll give you some suggestions for where to turn if you want a more thorough exploration of the subject.

At a very basic level, curiosity cabinets are a physical embodiment of our human tendency to collect. If you've ever gone for a walk and found yourself bringing home a shiny pebble or a beautiful feather or an interesting shell to set on your windowsill, you understand the impulse. Curiosity cabinets are that impulse taken to an elaborate extreme. They have their roots in Europe in the late 1400s and early 1500s.

This was a period of tremendous change and discovery. Explorers were encountering new lands and new peoples and coming home with dazzling treasures and fantastic accounts of their voyages. New trade routes were opening up, and cultures were coming into contact with each other for the first time. The world suddenly seemed like a bigger and more exciting place. Assembling curiosity cabinets helped people make sense of this expanding world.

Some of the earliest and most elaborate cabinets were owned by influential members of the aristocracy, nobility, and clergy. These powerful men amassed huge collections of the newly discovered wonders of the world. These collections were wide-ranging and indiscriminate. If an object was beautiful (like gemstones or pearls) or exotic (items of clothing from newly encountered people) or even just new (the shell from a freshly-discovered species of nautilus), it could find its way into a cabinet. Even gruesome objects (such as human skulls or malformed animals) had a place. Man-made items like statues and coins sat side by side with fossils, plants, and preserved animals. The collections could be housed in elaborate free-standing cupboards or could fill entire rooms. They were organized according to the whim of the collector and were seen as symbols of power and prestige.

During the 1600s and 1700s, these eclectic collections assembled to impress began to give way to more focused ones intended to enlighten and instruct. Instead of acquiring things because they were rare or expensive or exotic and then displaying them at random, collectors began to specialize and systematize. Someone might set out to gather together every kind of South American bird or every mollusk found in European waters or every African beetle. There was a move away from rarity and toward completeness. These new sorts of collections demanded a new method of organization. Objects no longer sat mixed together on shelves. Instead they were carefully arranged in a way that both displayed the item and helped put the relationships between them in a larger context.

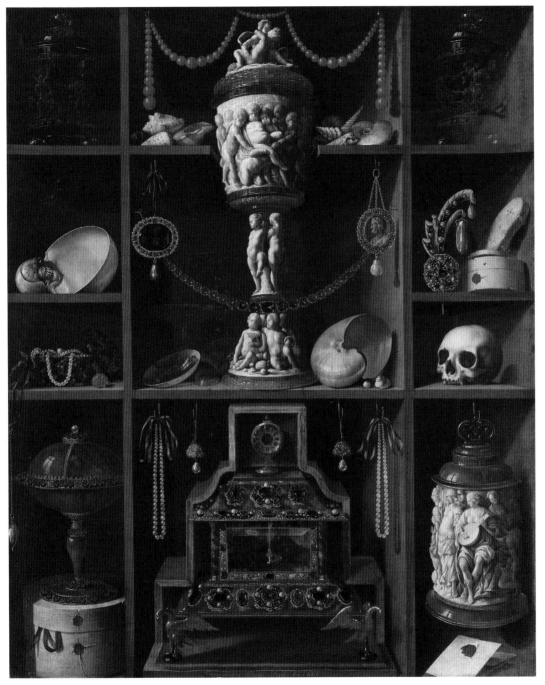

An eclectic cabinet show-
casing beautiful treasures
beside disquieting remind-
ers of mortality and
featuring both natural
and man-made objects.
Painted by Johann Georg
Hinz (also spelled Hainz or
Hintz), a baroque painter
from Hamburg, around
1666. Image courtesy
of the Hamburg
Kunsthalle, provided
by Art Resource, NY.
All rights reserved.

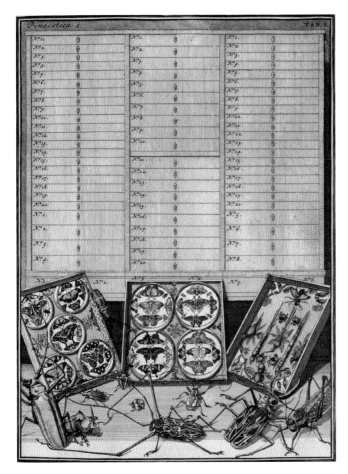

Dutch merchant Levinus Vincent amassed one of the most extensive cabinets of his time and made it available to visitors and scholars. He documented his collection in Wondertooneel der Nature, *a two-volume catalog published in 1706 and 1715. This image from the second volume shows a portion of his collection of insects.*

absolutely did not go outside and flip over rocks and catch bugs and poke at rotted logs. Expertise came from a deep knowledge of ancient texts, not from first-hand knowledge of the world.

Somewhere along the way, that began to change. By the late 1600s, Robert Hooke, in his capacity as director of the Royal Society's repository of natural specimens, could say that it was "much to be wisht for and indeavoured that there might be made and kept in some Repository as full and compleat a Collection of all vareties of Natural Bodies as could be obtain'd where an Inquirer might be able to have recourse, where he might peruse, and turn over, and spell, and read the Book of Nature … The use of such a Collection is not for Divertisement, and Wonder and Gazing … but for the most serious and diligent study of the most able Proficient in Natural Philosophy." As cabinets evolved from jumbles of treasures to ordered ranks of specimens, they became a new place for people to study nature. A bug or a shell or a bone became a more authoritative source than a thousand-year-old book. It was now possible to learn about nature from the natural world itself, and curiosity cabinets were at the heart of that transition.

Just as the form and purpose of cabinets were changing, so were the groups of people who assembled them. Once the playthings of the wealthy and powerful, cabinets eventually became common among members of the middle class too. In the 1700s and 1800s, lawyers, doctors, and merchants (and even sometimes their wives and daughters) were all likely to have collections of their own. Popular books like William Kirby's *A Hand-book to the Order Lepidoptera* (from which came several of the prints used later in this book) included guidelines on how to catch your own butterflies, "it is hard work to run down a Butterfly, and, in general, it is unnecessary," how to purchase them, "undoubtedly the cheapest way of buying Butterflies is to buy miscellaneous lots at an auction," and how to store and display them, "the specimens are then arranged in the cabinet in rows, separated by pencil lines … the name of the genus is placed above them, and that of the species, written or printed smaller, below … four specimens of each species are required, to show the upper and under surfaces of both sexes; but it is better to have more as a row gives a much better idea of a species than a single specimen of each sex." Something that was once an ostentatious display of wealth and power grew into both a site of scientific inquiry and a popular pastime.

This transition in the content and structure of cabinets was a reflection of a larger shift in ideas the cabinets embodied and in notions of how knowledge was generated and shared. It seems odd to modern readers, but until well into the 1600s, if you wanted to learn about the natural world, you went to a university and you read what Aristotle and Pliny and Dioscorides and other ancient Greeks had written about it more than a thousand years ago. You

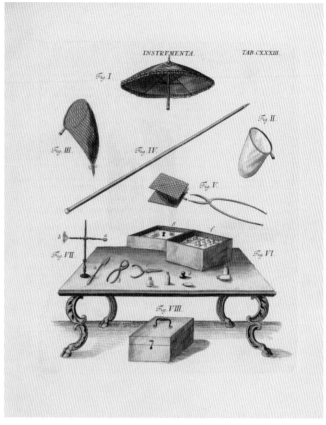

The account I've offered here has been shamefully brief. If you find you're interested in the subject, there are a host of excellent books available on curiosity cabinets. Arthur MacGregor's *Curiosity and Enlightenment: Collectors and Collections from the Sixteenth to the Nineteenth Century* is a marvelous place to start. Patrick Mauriès' book, *Cabinets of Curiosities*, is overflowing with amazing images and provides tremendous visual inspiration. And if you're looking for a truly immersive experience, the entire contents of Albertus Seba's *Cabinet of Natural Curiosities*, originally published in the 1700s, has been reprinted with an exceptional introduction by Irmgard Müsch. Richard Fortey speaks eloquently of the role of collections in science in his piece "Archives of Life: Science and Collections," published in *Seeing Further: The Story of Science, Discovery & the Genius of the Royal Society*.

Two plates from Jacob Christian Schäffer's introduction to entomology, Elementa Entomologica, *published in 1766. Schäffer had an impressive cabinet and assumed his readers would wish to assemble one of their own. He included a picture of an ornately decorated cabinet and of the assortment of tools and materials a collector would need to get started.*

PRINTS

There is a long tradition of making exquisitely detailed catalogs of the items in curiosity cabinets. Preparing these catalogs was a costly and complicated undertaking. Commissioning illustrations and overseeing printing involved substantial outlays of both time and money. But it became increasingly common and served several purposes.

As it was almost never possible to complete a collection (collectors are rarely sated), an illustration of an item held by a fellow collector could serve as a placeholder and fill in the gaps in another collection. Illustrations also captured aspects of items that were difficult to preserve. Plant and animal specimens degraded over time while pictures remained vibrant. Perhaps most importantly, as interest in the subject grew, published catalogs of cabinets made their contents accessible to people who could never hope to visit them in person.

I would have loved to work with images from some of these early catalogs. They were small works of art. They were also costly and usually published in very small numbers. The intervening years have made them both rarer and more expensive. The few originals I could find for sale were well out of my price range. Just as important, not all of them lent themselves to being adapted as knitting patterns. I could have worked from reproductions. Several of the catalogs have been reproduced in modern editions, and many of the others are available in digital versions. But I wanted to work from the originals, from something I could hold in my hands.

The joy of collecting is a fundamental part of the appeal of curiosity cabinets, and I admit that a bit of this collector's impulse influenced my desire to actually own the images I used in the book. So I turned to a slightly more available resource, prints from works of natural history. These were very much inspired by the same spirit of exploration and classification that lay behind curiosity cabinets but tended to be printed in larger numbers. They also included even more specimens. This meant that I had a wider array of images to choose from and that I could afford to indulge my desire to own the pieces I worked with. I hope you will forgive me this small lapse.

Vanessa antiopa, *Lycaena virgaureae*, *Polyommatus argiolus*, and *Polyommatus corydon* are from Volume 29 of *The Naturalist's Library*. This forty-volume series was produced and edited by Scottish naturalist William Jardine between 1833 and 1843. The series contains fourteen volumes of birds, thirteen of mammals, six of fish, and seven of insects. The individual volumes were each prepared by experts in their fields. The beautifully illustrated and inexpensively bound books were hugely popular and helped make natural history accessible to large portions of Victorian society.

The four prints used here come from the third of the seven books focused on entomology. It was written by James Duncan and published in 1835. It is devoted to British butterflies (a later volume by Duncan focused on butterflies of other lands). The book's goal was to offer "as complete a manual of the Diurnal Lepidoptera of our own country, as was possible in the space to which we have judged it advisable to limit the subject."

Delias eucharis, *Erasmia pulchella*, *Smerinthus ocellatus*, *Metopsilus porcellus*, and *Danima banksiae* are from Volumes 2, 3, and 4 of *A Hand-book to the Order Lepidoptera*, part of the Lloyd's Natural History series. Just as Jardine prepared an encyclopedia of natural history in the 1830s and 40s, English zoologist Richard Bowdler Sharpe did much the same in the 1890s. This sixteen-volume set covers butterflies and moths (five volumes), British birds (four volumes), primates and game birds (two volumes each), and carnivores, marsupials, and British mammals (one volume each).

The five volumes on moths and butterflies were prepared by English entomologist William Forsell Kirby and published in 1896 and 1897. Rather than splitting butterflies into British and non-British groups as Duncan had done, Kirby structured his volume so that "our native species of Butterflies are described and figured, and at the same time a review of their exotic relatives is attempted." He initially thought this would take only two or perhaps three volumes, but the collection quickly grew to five.

And yes, several of the plates used here do show moths. I promise they're the friendly, well-behaved sorts of moths, and their off-spring would much prefer to feast on tasty plants than on your stash!

TIPS

This book doesn't teach you how to knit. I assume you already know the basics (how to knit and purl, how to increase and decrease, and how to work flat and in the round). If you've got those things down, you can make any of these projects.

That said, there are a few little things that might be useful to know ahead of time. Most of these are fairly standard knitting pattern conventions, so if you want to skip ahead to the patterns, please feel free. But if you happen find yourself with a question, you might want to come back here and see if some of this information helps. Topics are organized in alphabetical order to help you quickly find exactly what you're looking for.

Abbreviations: See the stitch key for a complete list of all the abbreviations used in the text of the patterns.

Cast on: Use any stretchy cast on you like. All of the projects shown in the pictures were made with the long-tailed cast on or a provisional cast on. If you have a personal favorite, feel free to use it instead.

Cast off: Use any stretchy cast off you like. Jeny's Surprisingly Stretchy Bind Off, as described in the Fall 2009 issue of *Knitty*, is a good choice for most projects.

Charts: All of these patterns use at least one chart. Charts are easy to work with, but they do require a bit of attention if you've not used them before. The important thing to remember is that charts show you a stylized picture of what the right side of your knitting will look like.

If you're working in the round, the right side of your fabric is always facing you, so the chart always shows you exactly what to do. Just read each row of the chart from right to left and make the stitch indicated in the right-side instructions in the stitch key.

If you're working back and forth, the procedure is a bit different. When you're working a right-side row, read that row of the chart from right to left and make the stitch indicated in the right-side instructions in the stitch key. When you're working a wrong-side row, read that row of the chart from left to right and make the stitch indicated in the wrong-side instructions in the stitch key.

Chart notes: Some of the charts include notes to draw your attention to particular features or help you with potential trouble spots. Please be sure to read these notes carefully before you begin.

Gauge: Adjusting your gauge is one of the easiest ways to fine tune the size of your finished object. This can be a bit risky if you're making something closely fitted like a sweater (it works, you just need to do a fair bit of planning and some math). But it's a perfectly reasonable approach for most of the projects in this book. Though if you try it, it is helpful to keep a few things in mind.

First, always remember that the finished size of a particular bit of knitting at any given spot is is going to be (more or less) the total number of stitches at that spot divided by the gauge. So if you've cast on 72 stitches for a sock, and you're getting a gauge of 9 stitches per inch, you divide 72 stitches by 9 stitches per inch to get size of 8 inches. For this to work, it's important that you're measuring your gauge over the stitch pattern you're using and over a blocked swatch (if you're going to block the finished object). This is a very handy bit of math and it gives you a tremendous amount of flexibility in substituting yarns or in adjusting the size of a finished object.

Second, adjusting the gauge of your socks requires a bit more thought than adjusting the gauge of your shawl or your cowl. Socks have to deal with some rather demanding conditions. The single best thing you can do to ensure the longevity of your socks is knit tightly enough that you get a firm fabric *in your chosen yarn*. That means if you've picked a thin sock yarn, you may need to knit at 9 or 9.5 stitches per inch. By the same token, if you've picked a thick sock yarn, you may be able to knit at 7.5 or 7 stitches per inch.

If you've selected a yarn that works best at a gauge different from that listed in the pattern, you should do a bit of math to figure out which of the sizes will work best for you. The easiest way to understand this is with an example. Say you've decided to make the *Smerinthus ocellatus* socks, and that your foot is about 8.5 inches around. This sock comes in four sizes (56, 64, 72, and 80 stitches), and it calls for a gauge of 8 stitches per inch.

If you're using a yarn that gives you a good sock fabric at 8 stitches per inch, you should make the 64-stitch size (64 stitches divided by 8 stitches per inch gives an 8-inch sock, which will fit an 8.5-inch foot).

If you're using a yarn that gives you a good sock fabric at 7 stitches per inch, the 64-stitch size won't work (64 stitches divided by 7 stitches per inch gives a sock a little over 9 inches, which would be too big). Instead, you need to make the 56-stitch size (56 stitches divided by 7 stitches per inch gives an 8-inch sock, which will fit an 8.5-inch foot).

If you're using a yarn that gives you a good sock fabric at 9 stitches per inch, the 64-stitch size won't work (64 stitches divided by 9 stitches per inch gives a sock a little over 7 inches around, which would be too small). Instead you need to make the 72-stitch size (72 stitches divided by 9 stitches per inch gives an 8-inch sock, which will fit an 8.5-inch foot).

The general guideline is, if you've chosen a *thicker* yarn and are getting *fewer* stitches per inch than what the pattern calls for, consider making a smaller size. If you've chosen a *thinner* yarn and are getting *more* stitches per inch than what the pattern calls for, consider making a larger size. But you should always double check the math to make sure that it will work for you.

Grafting: Graft the ends of your toes however you like. All of the projects shown in the pictures were grafted with kitchener stitch.

Heel flaps: Heel flaps are worked back and forth over somewhere around half of the stitches of the sock. Each sock pattern lists the specific stitches that are to be used for the heel flap. Be sure to read carefully to see which stitches to use.

It is easy to adjust the height of your heel flap to make your sock really fit your foot. To figure out the right height, try slipping a rubber band around your ankle, standing up, and rolling it as far down as it will go. Make sure it's straight and measure from the bottom of the rubber band to the floor. Try making your heel flap just a bit shorter than that measurement. Just be sure to work an even number of rows so you're lined up properly to continue with the heel turn.

Pattern repeats: Generally, a chart shows one full repeat of a stitch pattern. Unless otherwise noted, this stitch pattern is worked across or around the entire row or round of the piece.

For example, the Main Chart for the *Smerinthus ocellatus* sock is 8 stitches wide. The sock itself is 56, 64, 72, or 80 stitches around, depending on the size you're making. When the pattern tells you to "work the Main Chart once," that means repeat the 8 stitches of row 1 of the Main Chart 7, 8, 9, or 10 times to use up all 56, 64, 72, or 80 stitches of the round. Then repeat the 8 stitches of row 2 of the Main Chart 7, 8, 9, or 10 times to use up all 56, 64, 72, or 80 stitches of the round. Continue in this fashion until all rows have been worked.

Put another way, "work the chart" means repeat the stitches of the chart over and over across the entire row or round until you reach the end.

Needles: All the patterns are written to work with any style of needle. You can use double points, one circular, two circulars, or anything else you can come up with, and you can arrange your stitches across your needles however you like. The only thing to keep in mind is that you will occasionally be told to work on certain stitches while setting others aside (for example when you make a heel flap). When this happens, just count from the beginning of the row or round to find the required stitches and rearrange as needed.

Notes: Several of the patterns include special notes. These are intended to draw your attention to important aspects of the patterns. Please be sure to read these notes carefully before you begin.

Right side: The right side of your knitting is the outside or the public side. It is abbreviated RS throughout the text.

Shaded stitches: Some charts use shading to draw your attention to certain stitches. When this happens, there will always be a note explaining the specific instructions for that particular pattern. Please be sure to read these notes carefully before you begin.

Sizing: Each of the patterns is offered in at least two sizes. Sometimes stitch counts or pattern repeats or other instructions differ from one size to the next. This is indicated by first giving the stitch count or pattern repeat for the smallest size and then giving the stitch count or pattern repeat for the larger sizes in square brackets. If there is more than one larger size, the stitch counts or pattern repeats will be separated by commas. So the instruction "Cast on 24 [36, 48] stitches" means cast on 24 stitches if you are making the smallest size, cast on 36 stitches if you are making the medium size, and cast on 48 stitches if you are making the largest size.

Sometimes sizing is indicated on the charts by shading certain squares. When this happens, there will always be a note explaining the specific instructions for that particular pattern. Please be sure to read these notes carefully before you begin.

Stitch key: The stitch key gives the symbol, the name, the abbreviation if needed, and the instructions for each stitch or group of stitches. When needed, it also gives the instructions for working a particular stitch on the wrong side of the fabric. Be sure to follow these wrong-side instructions when working a wrong-side row.

Slipped stitches: Many of the projects call for slipping stitches along the edge of the knitting to create a tidy selvage stitch. There are almost as many ways to do this as there are knitters. As long

as you are getting elongated stitches along the edge of the fabric, you're doing it right!

One approach that works for most people is to always slip the first stitch as if to purl with your yarn held to the wrong side of the fabric. If you find that's not working for the way you knit, you can also try holding the yarn to the back of the work and slipping as if to knit on right-side rows and holding the yarn to the front of the work and slipping as if to purl on wrong-side rows.

Stitch markers: Most patterns suggest using a stitch marker to indicate the beginning of the round. This is optional, but it can make it easier to see exactly what you are doing. If you find them helpful, you may also wish to use stitch markers to separate pattern repeats or to divide the front and back of a sock.

Toes: Several of the socks have a bit of ribbing or other patterning on the toes. If you find that bothers your toes, you can always substitute stockinette or reversed stockinette instead.

It is easy to adjust the shape of the toes to fit your feet. Most of the socks here have you decrease every other row until half your decreases are done and then decrease every round. If you've got pointy toes, you may want to decrease every other round until closer to three quarters of your decreases are done. If you've got flatter toes, you may want to decrease every other round until only one quarter of your decreases are done.

Wrong side: The wrong side of your knitting is the inside or the private side. It is abbreviated WS throughout the text.

Yarn requirements: Each pattern lists the approximate yardage used for the project shown. This is a good guideline, but estimating yardage requirements is a bit of a black art. If you decide to make the leg of your sock 10 inches tall or to make your fingerless gloves elbow length, you're going to need more yarn. When in doubt, buy extra! It's much easier to return an unneeded skein (or add it to the stash) than to run out on the last row.

STITCH KEY

Single Stitches

Symbol	Right Side	Wrong Side	Abbreviation
|	Knit.	Purl.	k
⟊	Knit through the back loop.	Purl through the back loop.	ktbl
⟀	Knit, wrapping the yarn around the needle twice.		
—	Purl.	Knit.	p
⟋	Purl through the back loop.	Knit through the back loop.	ptbl
○	Yarn over.	Yarn over.	yo
→	Slip: Slip as if to purl with yarn to inside or wrong side of object.	Slip as if to purl with yarn to inside or wrong side of object.	sl
▩	No stitch: Indicates a square on the chart that does not correspond to a stitch. Do nothing. Proceed to the next chart symbol.		

Single Decreases

Symbol	Right Side	Wrong Side	Abbreviation
	Right-leaning knit decrease: Knit 2 together.	Purl 2 together.	k2tog
	Right-leaning purl decrease: Purl 2 together.		p2tog
	Right-leaning twisted knit decrease: Slip 1 knitwise. Slip another 1 knitwise. Return the slipped stitches to the left needle. Knit 2 together.	Slip 1 knitwise. Slip another 1 knitwise. Return the slipped stitches to the left needle. Purl 2 together.	
	Left-leaning knit decrease: Slip 1 knitwise. Slip another 1 knitwise. Return slipped stitches to the left needle. Insert the right needle from the right to the left into the back loops of both stitches. Knit both together.	Slip 1 knitwise. Slip another 1 knitwise. Return slipped stitches to the left needle. Purl 2 together through the back loops.	ssk
	Left-leaning purl decrease: Slip 1 knitwise. Slip another 1 knitwise. Return slipped stitches to the left needle. Purl 2 together through the back loops.		ssp
	Left-leaning twisted knit decrease: Insert the right needle from the right to the left into the back loops of 2 stitches. Knit both together.	Purl 2 together through the back loops.	
	Slipped decrease: Knit 2. Using your left needle tip, grab the first stitch you worked and slip it over the second one and off the needle.		

Double Decreases

Symbol	Right Side
⟨right-leaning double decrease symbol⟩	Right-leaning double knit decrease: Slip 1 knitwise. Slip another 1 knitwise. Return slipped stitches to the left needle. Insert the right needle from the right to the left into the back loops of both stitches. Knit both together. Put the resulting stitch back on the left needle. Pass the second stitch on the left needle over the first. Slip the first stitch back to the right needle.
⟨left-leaning double decrease symbol⟩	Left leaning-double knit decrease: Slip 1 knitwise. Knit 2 together. Pass slipped stitch over.
⟨centered double decrease symbol⟩	Centered double knit decrease: Slip 2 together at the same time as if to knit 2 together. Knit 1. Pass the slipped stitches over.

Single Increases

Symbol	Right Side
⟨make 1 right knitwise symbol⟩	Make 1 right knitwise: With the left needle, lift the strand of yarn between the last stitch you worked and the stitch you would normally work next from the back to the front. Knit into the loop created by the strand of yarn you just picked up.
⟨make 1 right purlwise symbol⟩	Make 1 right purlwise: With the left needle, lift the strand of yarn between the last stitch you worked and the stitch you would normally work next from the back to the front. Purl into the loop created by the strand of yarn you just picked up.
⟨make 1 left knitwise symbol⟩	Make 1 left knitwise: With the left needle, lift the strand of yarn between the last stitch you worked and the stitch you would normally work next from the front to the back. Knit into the back of the loop created by the strand of yarn you just picked up.
⟨make 1 left purlwise symbol⟩	Make 1 left purlwise: With the left needle, lift the strand of yarn between the last stitch you worked and the stitch you would normally work next from the front to the back. Purl into the back of the loop created by the strand of yarn you just picked up.

Multiple Stitches

Symbol	Right Side
⌐‖‖‖ ○	Yarn over cluster: Yarn over. Knit 3. Using your left needle tip, grab the yarn over over and slip it over the 3 knit stitches and off the needle.
‖‖‖ ╱⌐	1x3 Cable, right: Slip 3 to cable needle, hold in back, knit 1, knit 3 from cable needle.
‖‖ ╱‖‖	2x2 Cable, right: Slip 2 to cable needle, hold in back, knit 2, knit 2 from cable needle.
⌐╱⟨— —⟩╲⌐	1x2x1 Cable, right: Slip 3 to cable needle, hold in back, knit 1 through the back loop. Slip the 3 stitches on the cable needle back to the left needle. Slip 1 to cable needle, hold in front, purl 2, knit 1 through the back loop from cable needle.
‖‖ ╱ⓌⓌ	1x2 Cable, right, double wrap: Slip 2 to cable needle, hold in back, knit 1 wrapping the yarn around the needle twice, knit 2 from cable needle.
⌐╲‖‖‖	1x3 Cable, left: Slip 1 to cable needle, hold in front, knit 3, knit 1 from cable needle.
⌐ ╲‖‖	2x2 Cable, left: Slip 2 to cable needle, hold in frong, knit 2, knit 2 from cable needle.
⌐╱⟨— —⟩╲⌐	1x2x1 Cable, left: Slip 1 to cable needle, hold in front. Slip 2 to second cable needle, hold in back. Knit 1 through the back loop, purl 2 from second cable needle, knit 1 through the back loop from first cable needle.
ⓌⓌ╲‖‖	1x2 Cable, left, double wrap: Slip 1 to cable needle, hold in front, knit 2, knit 1 wrapping the yarn around the needle twice from cable needle.
⌐╲⌐	1x1 Cable, left: Slip 1 to cable needle, hold in front, knit 1, knit 1 from cable needle.

STITCH KEY ∼ 15

VANESSA ANTIOPA

The upper side of both wings is a uniform deep
purplish-brown, having the appearance of velvet,
bounded externally by a broad band of velvet-black, in
which are placed a series of pretty large violet-blue spots
... beyond this there is a broad cream-coloured border,
slightly waved on the inner side ... The anterior border
has two cream-coloured spots beyond the middle,
and is mottled with yellow towards the base.

James Duncan

PLATE 18.

1. *Vanessa Io.*   2. *Vanessa Antiopa.*
    Peacock B.   *Camberwell beauty.*

VANESSA ANTIOPA SOCK

Shown in: Solemate by Lorna's Laces in the color Magnificent Mile. Made in size Medium with about 300 yards of yarn.
Gauge and sizing: 8 stitches in 1 inch in stockinette. Fits a foot or leg of about 7.5 [8.5, 9.5] inches.

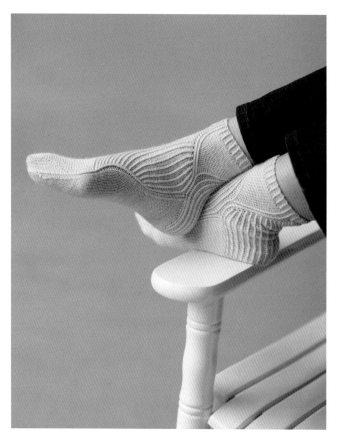

Cast on: Cast on 56 [64, 72] stitches. Place marker and join for working in the round.

Cuff and leg: Work row 1 of the appropriate Leg Chart 8 times. Work the rest of the appropriate Leg Chart once. Repeat the last row of the appropriate Leg Chart until sock reaches desired height.

Heel flap: The heel flap is worked over stitches 30-56 [34-64, 38-72]. It uses 27 [31, 35] stitches.

Row 1 is a wrong-side row (worked with the inside of the sock facing you). Row 2 is a right-side row (worked with the outside of the sock facing you). Work these 2 rows 13 [15, 17] times or until heel flap reaches desired length.

Row 1 (WS): Sl1, (k1, sl1) 12 [14, 16] times, k1, p1.
Row 2 (RS): Sl1, p1, (ktbl1, p1) 12 [14, 16] times, k1.

Heel turn: Odd rows are wrong-side rows (worked with the inside of the sock facing you). Even rows are right-side rows (worked with the outside of the sock facing you). Turn at the end of each row.

Row 1 (WS): Sl1, p15 [17, 19], p2tog, p1.
Row 2 (RS): Sl1, k6, ssk, k1.
Row 3 (WS): Sl1, p7, p2tog, p1.
Row 4 (RS): Sl1, k8, ssk, k1.

Row 5 (WS): Sl1, p9, p2tog, p1.
Row 6 (RS): Sl1, k10, ssk, k1.
Row 7 (WS): Sl1, p11, p2tog, p1.
Row 8 (RS): Sl1, k12, ssk, k1.
Row 9 (WS): Sl1, p13, p2tog, p1.
Row 10 (RS): Sl1, k14, ssk, k1.

For Medium and Large, as above plus:
Row 11 (WS): Sl1, p15, p2tog, p1.
Row 12 (RS): Sl1, k16, ssk, k1.

For Large, as above plus:
Row 13 (WS): Sl1, p17, p2tog, p1.
Row 14 (RS): Sl1, k18, ssk, k1.

17 [19, 21] stitches remain.

Gusset and foot:
Setup round: Pick up and knit stitches along the side of the heel flap, place first marker. Work across the top of the foot following the first row of the appropriate Foot Chart, place second marker. Pick up and knit stitches along the other side of the heel flap, k8 [9, 10]. The round now begins in the middle of the bottom of the foot.

Decrease round: K until 3 stitches remain before first marker, k2tog, k1. Work across the top of the foot following the first row of the appropriate Foot Chart. K1, ssk, k to end of round. 2 stitches decreased.

Non-decrease round A: K to first marker. Work across the top of the foot following the first row of the appropriate Foot Chart. K to end of round.

Alternate decrease and non-decrease A rounds until 58 [66, 74] stitches remain. You will be repeating the first row of the appropriate Foot Chart through all the gusset decreases. You will begin working through the rest of the appropriate Foot Chart in the next section.

Non-decrease round B: K to first marker. Work across the top of the foot following the next row of the appropriate Foot Chart. K to end of round.

Work non-decrease round B until you reach the final row of the appropriate Foot Chart. Repeat the final row of the appropriate Foot Chart until sock measures 2 [2.25, 2.5] inches shorter than desired length.

Toe:
Decrease round: K until 3 stitches remain before first marker, k2tog, k1. P1, work a left-leaning twisted decrease, p until 3 stitches remain before second marker, work a right-leaning twisted decrease, p1. K1, ssk, k to end of round. 4 stitches decreased.

Non-decrease round: K to first marker. P1, ktbl1, p until 2 stitches remain before second marker, ktbl1, p1. K to end of round.

Work these 2 rounds 4 [6, 8] times, 42 stitches remain. Work the decrease round 6 more times, 18 stitches remain. K to marker. Remove markers. Graft toes. Weave in ends.

Stitch Key

⟑	Knit through the back loop
—	Purl
O	Yarn over
⟋	Right-leaning twisted knit decrease
⟍	Left-leaning twisted knit decrease
(light square)	Work for Medium and Large
(gray square)	Work for Large

Chart notes: The left and right socks use different charts. Be sure to follow the appropriate charts.

Left Leg Chart

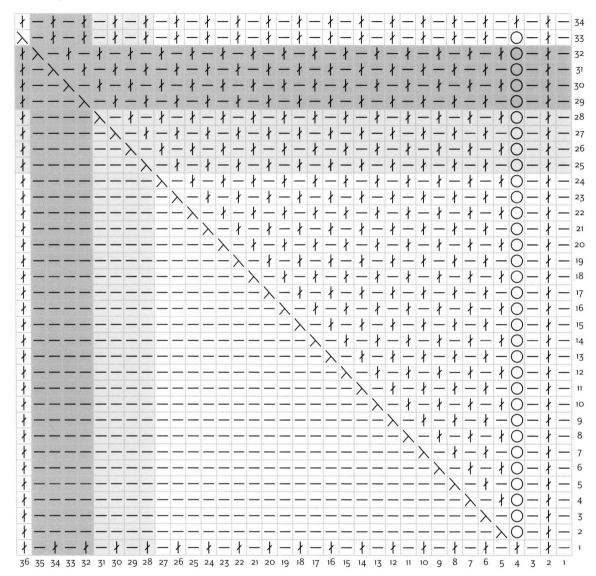

Chart notes: The shaded stitches are used to adjust sizing. On all charts, work only the unshaded stitches for size Small. Work the unshaded stitches and the light gray stitches for size Medium. Work all stitches for size Large.

Right Leg Chart

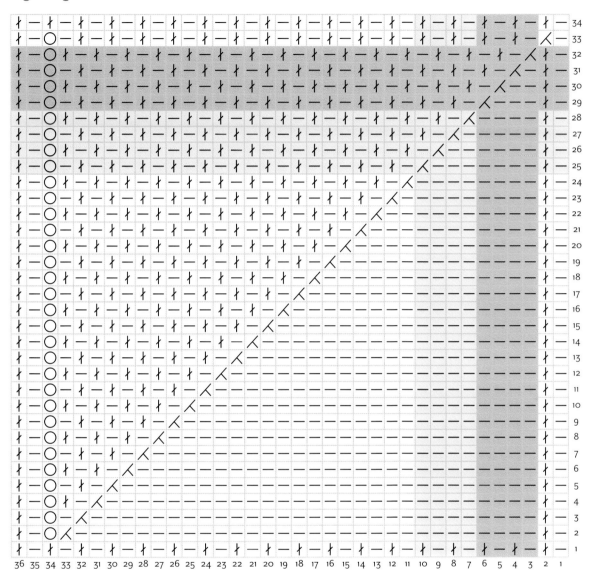

Left Foot Chart

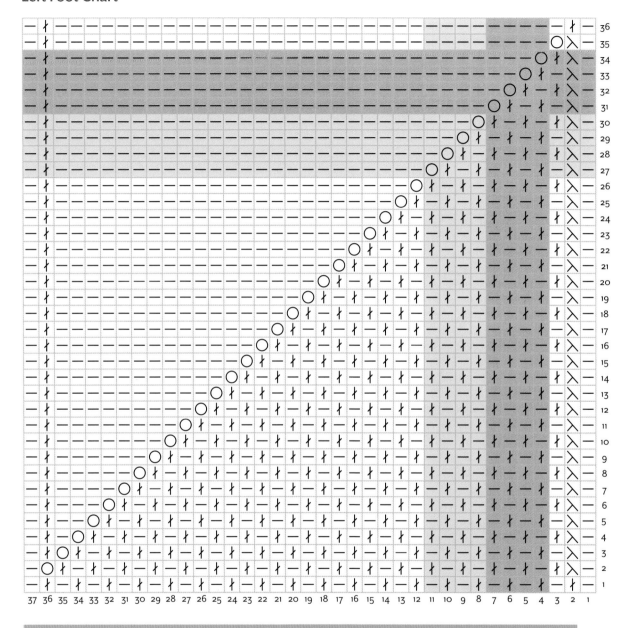

Chart notes: The shaded stitches are used to adjust sizing. On all charts, work only the unshaded stitches for size Small. Work the unshaded stitches and the light gray stitches for size Medium. Work all stitches for size Large.

Right Foot Chart

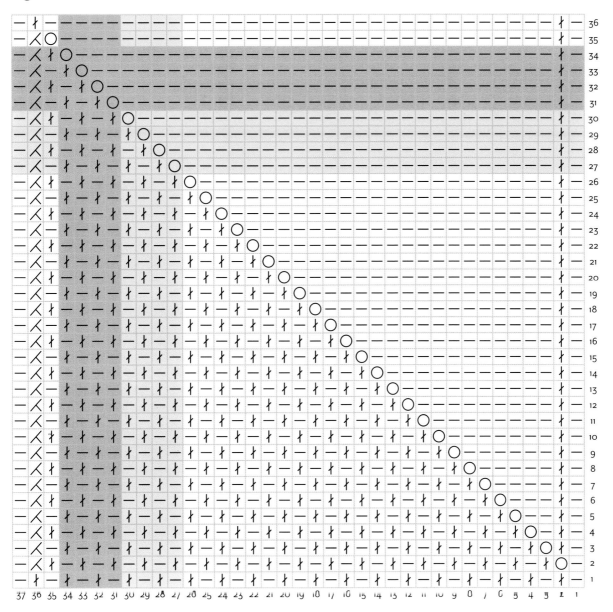

VANESSA ANTIOPA COWL

Shown in: Lion and Lamb by Lorna's Laces in the color Hermosa. Made in size Medium with about 150 yards of yarn.

Gauge and sizing: 14 stitches in 4 inches in pattern as charted. After blocking, the cowl is about 22 [26, 30] inches long. Height is adjustable, shown here at 10 inches.

Notes: This simple cowl (it's really just a rectangle) is surprisingly versatile and can be worn a number of ways. Both sides of the stitch are lovely, and the holes in the fabric make perfect buttonholes.

All the interest comes in how you fasten it! Try securing it (partially folded over looks great) with a pretty pin or lacing it up with a ribbon. You can even make your own double-sided buttons (see page 28) to hold it in place. Of course, if that sounds too daunting, you can just sew regular buttons on one narrow end instead.

Cast on: Cast on 79 [93, 107] stitches.

Body: Odd rows are wrong-side rows (worked with the inside of the cowl facing you, following the wrong-side notations in the stitch key, and reading the chart from left to right). Even rows are right-side rows (worked with the outside of the cowl facing you, following the right-side notations in the stitch key, and reading the chart from right to left).

Work row 1 of the Main Chart once. Work rows 2 and 3 until cowl reaches desired height (shown here worked 32 times). Stop after completing row 3 of the Main Chart. Work row 4 of the Main Chart once.

Finishing: Bind off loosely. Weave in ends. Block vigorously.

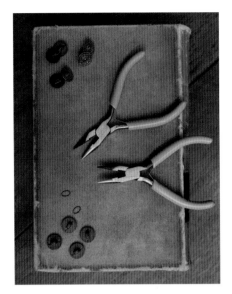

1) Supplies: jump rings, shank buttons, two pairs of needle nosed pliers.

2) Grasp the jump ring with the pliers, being sure the opening in the ring is between the pliers.

3) Gently twist the ring open.

4) Thread two buttons onto the ring.

5) Gently twist the ring closed.

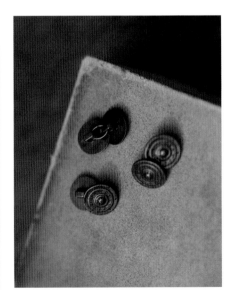

6) Finished buttons.

Stitch Key

| | RS: Knit
WS: Purl

— RS: Purl
WS: Knit

→ Slip as if to purl

○ Yarn over

╱ Right-leaning knit decrease

╲ Left-leaning knit decrease

⋀ Centered double knit decrease

☐ Work these stitches 5 [6, 7] times

Main Chart

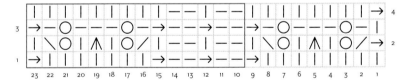

Chart notes: The stitches surrounded by the red border are repeated to adjust the size of the cowl. Work them 5 [6, 7] times.

LYCAENA VIRGAUREAE

The male [is] brilliant copper colour above,

inclining to yellow, the wings margined externally with

black, and the hinder pair having a few black spots near

the posterior edge. On the underside, the primary wings

are pale yellow ... and the hinder margin is clouded

with dusky; the secondary wings are dusky towards

the base ... The wings of the female are thickly

spotted and clouded with black above.

James Duncan

PLATE 29.

1. *Lycaena dispar, Male* 2. *Female*   3. *Lycaena Virgaureae*
Large Copper.   Scarce Copper.

LYCAENA VIRGAUREAE SOCK

Shown in: BFL Luxe Blend by Black Bunny Fibers in the color Hedgehog's Nose. Made in size Small with about 300 yards of yarn.
Gauge and sizing: 8.5 stitches in 1 inch in stockinette. Fits a foot or leg of about 7.5 [8.5, 9.5, 10.5] inches.
Notes: The cuff and leg are worked with needles one size larger than those needed to get gauge. The fabric isn't terribly stretchy, so you will cast on more stitches than you might expect. I suggest trying the sock on after you've worked two repeats of the Main Chart to make sure it fits well.

Cast on: Using needles one size larger than those needed to get gauge, cast on 64 [72, 80, 88] stitches. Place marker and join for working in the round.

Cuff and leg: Using needles one size larger than those needed to get gauge, work the Cuff Chart 8 times. Work the appropriate Main Chart until sock reaches desired height. Stop after completing row 6 of the appropriate Main Chart.

Heel flap: The heel flap is worked over stitches 33-64 [37-72, 41-80, 45-88]. It uses 32 [36, 40, 44] stitches.

Odd rows are wrong-side rows (worked with the inside of the sock facing you, following the wrong-side notations in the stitch key, and reading the chart from left to right). Even rows are right-side rows (worked with the outside of the sock facing you, following the right-side notations in the stitch key, and reading the chart from right to left). Using needles needed to get gauge, work the Heel Chart 8 [9, 10, 11] times or until heel flap reaches desired length.

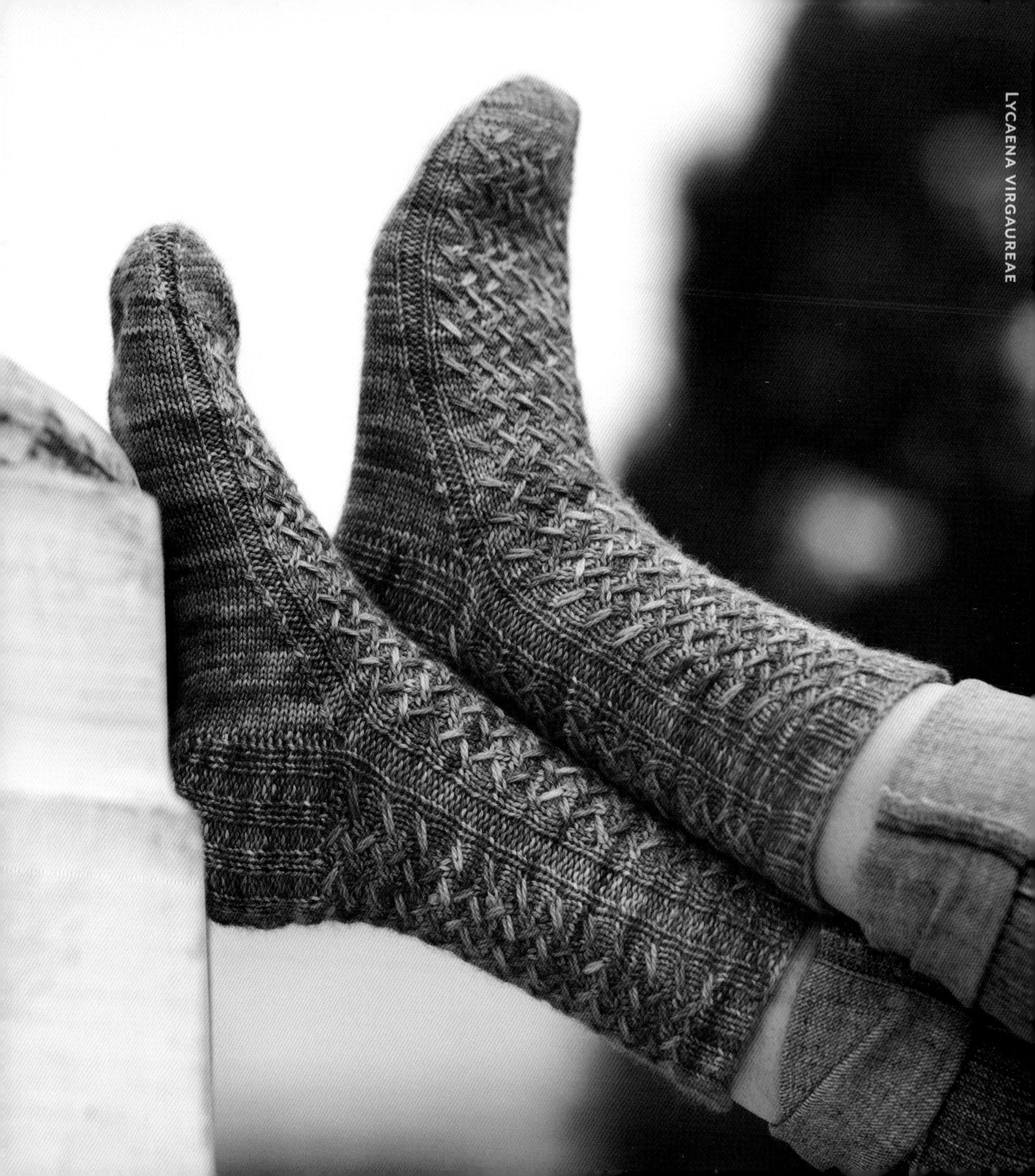

Heel turn: Odd rows are wrong-side rows (worked with the inside of the sock facing you). Even rows are right-side rows (worked with the outside of the sock facing you). Turn at the end of each row.

Row 1 (WS): Sl1, p18 [20, 22, 24] p2tog, p1.
Row 2 (RS): Sl1, k7, ssk, k1.
Row 3 (WS): Sl1, p8, p2tog, p1.
Row 4 (RS): Sl1, k9, ssk, k1.
Row 5 (WS): Sl1, p10, p2tog, p1.
Row 6 (RS): Sl1, k11, ssk, k1.
Row 7 (WS): Sl1, p12, p2tog, p1.
Row 8 (RS): Sl1, k13, ssk, k1.
Row 9 (WS): Sl1, p14, p2tog, p1.
Row 10 (RS): Sl1, k15, ssk, k1.
Row 11 (WS): Sl1, p16, p2tog, p1.
Row 12 (RS): Sl1, k17, ssk, k1.

For Medium, Large, and Extra Large, as above plus:
Row 13 (WS): Sl1, p18, p2tog, p1.
Row 14 (RS): Sl1, k19, ssk, k1.

For Large and Extra Large, as above plus:
Row 15 (WS): Sl1, p20, p2tog, p1.
Row 16 (RS): Sl1, k21, ssk, k1.

For Extra Large, as above plus:
Row 17 (WS): Sl1, p22, p2tog, p1.
Row 18 (RS): Sl1, k23, ssk, k1.

20 [22, 24, 26] stitches remain.

Gusset and foot:
Setup round: Pick up and knit stitches along the side of the heel flap, place first marker. Work across the top of the foot following the first row of the appropriate Main Chart, place second marker. Pick up and knit stitches along the other side of the heel flap, k10 [11, 12, 13]. The round now begins in the middle of the bottom of the foot.

Decrease round: K until 3 stitches remain before first marker, k2tog, p1. Work across the top of the foot following the next row of the appropriate Main Chart. P1, ssk, k to end of round. 2 stitches decreased.

Non-decrease round: K until 1 stitch remains before first marker, p1. Work across the top of the foot following the next row of the appropriate Main Chart. P1, k to end of round.

Alternate decrease and non-decrease rounds until 64 [72, 80, 88] stitches remain. Repeat the non-decrease round until sock measures 2 [2.25, 2.5, 2.75] inches shorter than desired length. Stop after completing row 3 or row 6 of the appropriate Main Chart.

Toe:
Decrease round: K until 3 stitches remain before first marker, k2tog, p1. P1, ssk, k until 3 stitches remain before second marker, k2tog, p1. P1, ssk, k to end of round. 4 stitches decreased.

Non-decrease round: K until 1 stitch remains before first marker, p1. P1, k until 1 stitch remains before second marker, p1. P1, k to end of round.

Work these 2 rounds 6 [8, 10, 12] times, 40 stitches remain. Work the decrease round 6 more times, 16 stitches remain. K to first marker. Remove markers. Graft toes. Weave in ends.

Stitch Key

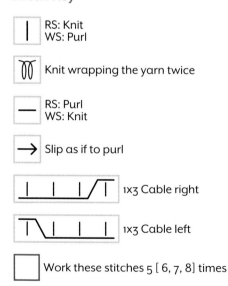

	RS: Knit WS: Purl
	Knit wrapping the yarn twice
	RS: Purl WS: Knit
	Slip as if to purl
	1x3 Cable right
	1x3 Cable left
	Work these stitches 5 [6, 7, 8] times

Cuff Chart

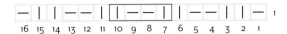

Left Main Chart

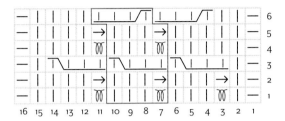

Heel Chart

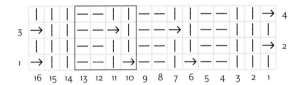

Right Main Chart

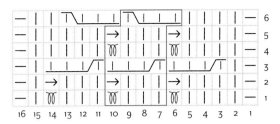

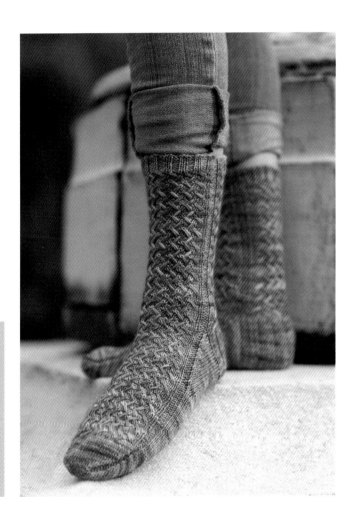

Chart notes: The left and right socks use different charts. Be sure to follow the appropriate charts.

One of the stitches in the chart tells you to knit, wrapping the yarn around the needle twice. When you come to this stitch in the next round, drop the extra loop of yarn off your needle.

The stitches surrounded by the red border are repeated to adjust the size of the sock. Work them 5 [6, 7, 8] times.

LYCAENA VIRGAUREAE SHAWL

Shown in: Devon by Black Bunny Fibers in the color Orange Marmalade. Made in size Medium with about 700 yards of yarn.
Gauge and sizing: 14 stitches in 3 inches in pattern as charted. Be sure to block your swatch before measuring. After blocking, the shawl is about 60 [66, 72] inches long. Height is adjustable, shown here at 24 inches.

Cast on: Cast on 284 [312, 340] stitches.

Bottom edge: Odd rows are right-side rows (worked with the outside of the shawl facing you, following the right-side notations in the stitch key, and reading the chart from right to left). Even rows are wrong-side rows (worked with the inside of the shawl facing you, following the wrong-side notations in the stitch key, and reading the chart from left to right).

Work the Main Chart 3 times. Work rows 1-6 of the Main Chart once more.

Body: Odd rows are right-side rows (worked with the outside of the shawl facing you, following the right-side notations in the stitch key, and reading the chart from right to left). Even rows are wrong-side rows (worked with the inside of the shawl facing you, following the wrong-side notations in the stitch key, and reading the chart from left to right).

Work the Body Chart until shawl reaches desired height (shown here worked 25 times). Stop after completing row 2 of the Body Chart.

Finishing: Bind off loosely, weave in ends. Block vigorously.

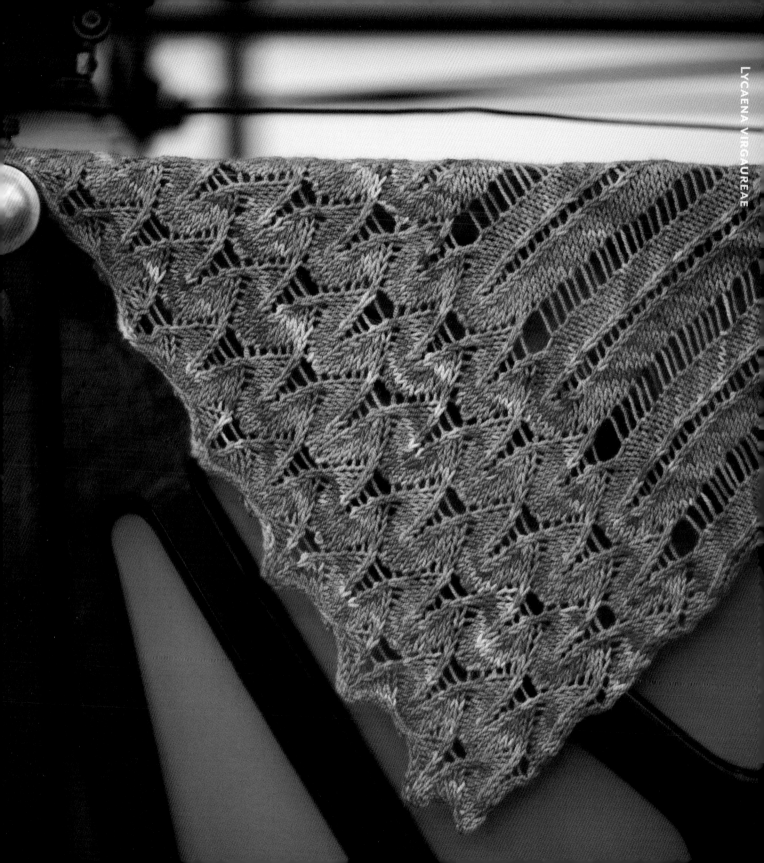

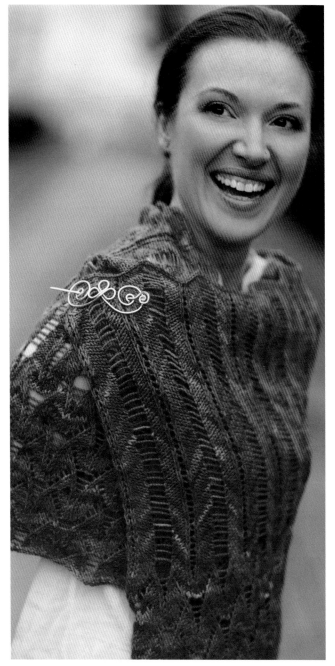

Stitch Key

| | RS: Knit
WS: Purl

→ Slip as if to purl

○ Yarn over

\ RS: Left-leaning knit decrease
WS: Left-leaning purl decrease

/ RS: Right-leaning knit decrease
WS: Right-leaning purl decrease

☐ Work these stitches 20 [22, 24] times

Main Chart

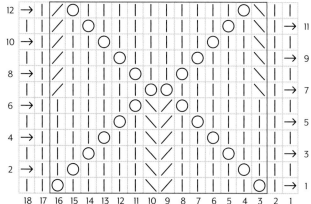

Body Chart

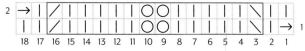

Chart notes: Work the double yarn overs on the Body Chart as follows: when you come to one, knit the first loop of the yarn over from the row below. Work two new yarn overs. Knit the next loop of the yarn over from the row below.

The stitches surrounded by the red border are repeated to adjust the size of the shawl. Work them 20 [22, 24] times.

POLYOMMATUS ARGIOLUS

The surface of the male [is] delicate light blue, slightly tinged with lilac, the wings narrowly edged behind with black; the female lighter blue above, with a broad dusky border in the primary wings, and a transverse series of spots of the same colour near the hinder edge of the secondary pair. Beneath, the colour is gray, faintly tinged with blue.

James Duncan

PLATE 31

1. *Polyommatus Argiolus*, Male. 2 Female   *Azure blue*.
3. _____ Alsus.   *Bedford blue*
4. _____ Acis.   *Mazarine blue*

POLYOMMATUS ARGIOLUS SOCK

Shown in: Arroyo by Malabrigo in the color Azules. Made in size Medium with about 350 yards of yarn.

Gauge and sizing: 8 stitches in 1 inch in stockinette. Fits a foot or leg of about 7.5 [8.5, 9.5, 10.5] inches.

Notes: The heel flap, gusset, foot, and toe directions are different for different sizes. Be sure to follow the appropriate directions.

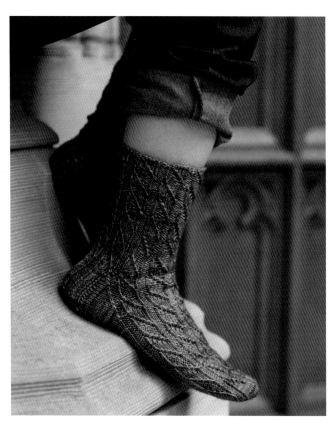

Cast on: Cast on 56 [64, 72, 80] stitches. Place marker and join for working in the round.

Cuff and leg: Work the appropriate Main Chart until sock reaches desired height. Stop after completing row 20 of the appropriate Main Chart.

Heel flap: For the Small and Large sizes only, you must shift your start of round marker back 1 stitch before you work the heel flap. To do this, the last time you work row 20 of the appropriate Main Chart, do not work the very last stitch of the round. That stitch (56 or 72 depending on the size you're making) is now the first stitch of your round. Shift your stitch marker to indicate this before you identify the stitches for your heel flap. The heel flap is worked over stitches 27-56 [33-64, 35-72, 41-80]. It uses a total of 30 [32, 38, 40] stitches.

Row 1 is a wrong-side row (worked with the inside of the sock facing you). Row 2 is a right-side row (worked with the outside of the sock facing you). Work these 2 rows 13 [15, 17, 19] times or until heel flap reaches desired length.

Small and Large:
Row 1 (WS): Sl1, p1, sl2, p1, ptbl1, k1, (k1, ptbl1, p1, sl2, p1, ptbl1, k1) 2 [3 times], k1, ptbl1, p1, sl2, p2.
Row 2 (RS): Sl1, k4, ktbl1, p1, (p1, ktbl1, k4, ktbl1, p1), 2 [3 times], p1, ktbl1, k5.

Medium and Extra Large:
Row 1 (WS): Sl1, ptbl1, p1, sl2, p1, ptbl1, k1, (k1, ptbl1, p1, sl2, p1, ptbl1, k1) 2 [3 times], k1, ptbl1, p1, sl2, p1, ptbl1, p1.
Row 2 (RS): Sl1, ktbl1, k4, ktbl1, p1, (p1, ktbl1, k4, ktbl1, p1), 2 [3 times], p1, ktbl1, k4, ktbl1, k1.

Heel turn: Odd rows are wrong-side rows (worked with the inside of the sock facing you). Even rows are right-side rows (worked with the outside of the sock facing you). Turn at the end of each row.

Row 1 (WS): Sl1, p16 [18, 20, 22], p2tog, p1.
Row 2 (RS): Sl1, k5 [7, 5, 7], ssk, k1.
Row 3 (WS): Sl1, p6 [8, 6, 8], p2tog, p1.
Row 4 (RS): Sl1, k7 [9, 7, 9], ssk, k1.
Row 5 (WS): Sl1, p8 [10, 8, 10], p2tog, p1.
Row 6 (RS): Sl1, k9 [11, 9, 11], ssk, k1.
Row 7 (WS): Sl1, p10 [12, 10, 12], p2tog, p1.
Row 8 (RS): Sl1, k11 [13, 11, 13], ssk, k1.
Row 9 (WS): Sl1, p12 [14, 12, 14], p2tog, p1.
Row 10 (RS): Sl1, k13 [15, 13, 15], ssk, k1.
Row 11 (WS): Sl1, k14 [16, 14, 16], p2tog, p1.
Row 12 (RS): Sl1, p15 [17, 15, 17], ssk, k1.

For Large and Extra Large, as above plus:
Row 13 (WS): Sl1, p— [—, 16, 18], p2tog, p1.
Row 14 (RS): Sl1, k— [—, 17, 19], ssk, k1.
Row 15 (WS): Sl1, p— [—, 18, 20], p2tog, p1.
Row 16 (RS): Sl1, k— [—, 19, 21], ssk, k1.

18 [20, 22, 24] stitches remain.

Gusset and foot:
Setup round: For the Small and Large sizes, pick up and knit 1 stitch in each of the slipped stitches along the side of the heel flap, place first marker. P1, work across the top of the foot following the first row of the appropriate Main Chart (you will work 3 [4] full repeats of the Main Chart), p1, place second marker. Pick up and knit 1 stitch in each of the slipped stitches along the other side of the heel flap, k9 [11]. The round now begins in the middle of the bottom of the foot.

For the Medium and Extra Large sizes, pick up and knit 1 stitch in each of the slipped stitches along the side of the heel flap, place first marker. Work across the top of the foot following the first row of the appropriate Main Chart (you will work 4 [5] full repeats of the Main Chart), place second marker. Pick up and knit 1 stitch in each of the slipped stitches along the other side of the heel flap, k10 [12]. The round now begins in the middle of the bottom of the foot.

Decrease round: For the Small and Large sizes, k until 3 stitches remain before first marker, k2tog, k1. P1, work across the top of the foot following the next row of the appropriate Main Chart (you will work 3 [4] full repeats of the Main Chart), p1. K1, ssk, k to end of round. 2 stitches decreased.

For the Medium and Extra Large sizes, k until 3 stitches remain before first marker, k2tog, p1. Work across the top of the foot following the next row of the appropriate Main Chart (you will work 4 [5] full repeats of the Main Chart). P1, ssk, k to end of round. 2 stitches decreased.

Non-decrease round: For the Small and Large sizes, k to first marker. P1, work across the top of the foot following the next row of the appropriate Main Chart (you will work 3 [4] full repeats of the Main Chart), p1. K to end of round.

For the Medium and Extra Large sizes, k until 1 stitch remains before first marker, p1. Work across the top of the foot following the next row of the appropriate Main Chart (you will work 4 [5] full repeats of the Main Chart). P1, k to end of round.

Alternate decrease and non-decrease rounds until 52 [64, 68, 80] stitches remain. Repeat the non-decrease round until sock measures 1.75 [2, 2.25, 2.5] inches shorter than desired length. Stop after completing row 10 or 20 of the appropriate Main Chart. Repeat row 1 or 11 of the appropriate Main Chart as needed to adjust length.

Toe:
Decrease round: For the Small and Large sizes, k until 3 stitches remain before first marker, k2tog, k1. P2, work a left-leaning twisted decrease, follow ribbing as established by row 1 of the appropriate Main Chart until 4 stitches remain before second marker, work a right-leaning twisted decrease, p2. K1, ssk, k to end of round. 4 stitches decreased.

For the Medium and Extra Large sizes, k until 3 stitches remain before first marker, k2tog, p1. P1, work a left-leaning twisted decrease, follow ribbing as established by row 1 of the appropriate Main Chart until 3 stitches remain before second marker, work a right-leaning twisted decrease, p1. P1, ssk, k to end of round. 4 stitches decreased.

Non-decrease round: For the Small and Large sizes, k to first marker. Follow ribbing as established by row 1 of the appropriate Main Chart to second marker. K to end of round. 4 stitches decreased.

For the Medium and Extra Large sizes, k until 1 stitch remains before first marker, p1. Follow ribbing as established by row 1 of the appropriate Main Chart to second marker. P1, k to end of round.

Work these 2 rounds 2 [5, 6 , 9] times, 44 stitches remain. Work the decrease round 7 more times, 16 stitches remain. K to marker. Remove markers. Graft toes. Weave in ends.

Stitch Key

| Knit

ʄ Knit through the back loop

— Purl

O Yarn over

⟋ Right-leaning twisted knit decrease

⟍ Left-leaning twisted knit decrease

Chart notes: The left and right socks use different charts. Be sure to follow the appropriate charts.

Left Main Chart

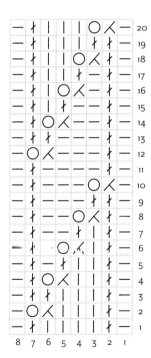

Right Main Chart

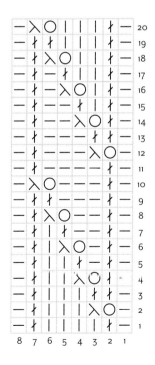

POLYOMMATUS ARGIOLUS MITT

Shown in: Sock by Malabrigo in the color Impressionist Sky. Made with a 34-inch long strip with about 150 yards of yarn.
Gauge and sizing: 7 stitches in 1 inch in stockinette. Fits any size arm, just make the strip as long as necessary.
Notes: You will need several safety pins and a crochet hook in a size similar to your needle size.

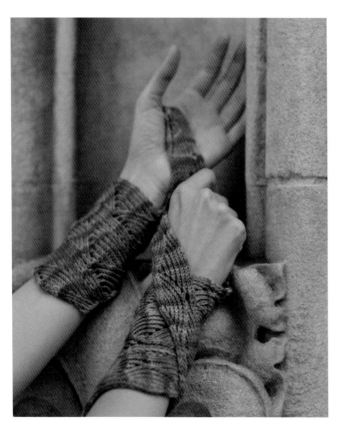

Cast on: Cast on 6 stitches. Leave a 3-yard tail (this will be used in finishing).

Strip: Odd rows are right-side rows (worked with the outside of the cuff facing you, following the right-side notations in the stitch key, and reading the chart from right to left). Even rows are wrong-side rows (worked with the inside of the cuff facing you, following the wrong-side notations in the stitch key, and reading the chart from left to right).

Work the appropriate Start Chart once. Work the appropriate Main Chart until strip reaches 28 inches. Try wrapping it around your wrist as shown in the pictures on page 50 to see how much more you need. Continue working the appropriate Main Chart until strip is 1 inch shorter than desired length. Stop after completing row 22 of the appropriate Main Chart. Work the appropriate End Chart once. Bind off. Leave a 2-yard tail (this will be used in finishing).

Finishing: Block the strips before seaming them together. Note that the edges of the strip have selvage stitches (made by the slipped stitch at the beginning of each row). You will use these selvage stitches to join the strip together.

When you wrap the strip, make a note of the point where the edges first join up by passing a safety pin through both selvage stitches to

mark them. To join the strip, pass a crochet hook through both of the selvage stitches. Wrap the tail you left at the cast on around the crochet hook and pull a loop of yarn through both of the selvage stitches.

Pass the crochet hook through the next two selvage stitches. Wrap the tail around the crochet hook and pull a loop of yarn through both of the selvage stitches and the previous stitch. Repeat until you've secured the first portion of the strip into a spiral making three full turns around your wrist. Continue to join for a few more stitches to bring the free end of the strip around the edge of your palm.

Put the cuff on and wrap the free end of the strip as shown in the pictures on page 50. Use several safety pins to carefully secure the strip and take the cuff off.

Use the tail you left when you bound off to sew the edge of the strip to the body of the cuff. Weave in ends.

Stitch Key

 RS: Knit through the back loop
WS: Purl through the back loop

 RS: Purl
WS: Knit

 Yarn over

 Slip as if to purl

 RS: Right-leaning twisted knit decrease
WS: Right-leaning twisted purl decrease

 RS: Left-leaning twisted knit decrease
WS: Left-leaning twisted purl decrease

Chart notes: The left and right mitts use different charts. Be sure to follow the appropriate charts.

Left Start Chart

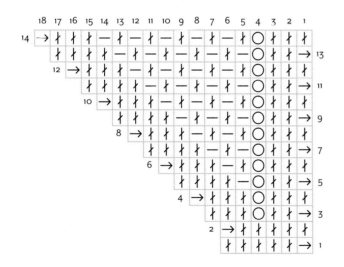

Right Start Chart

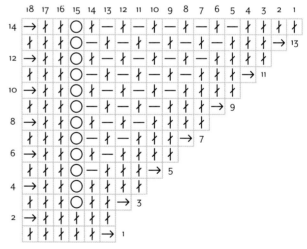

Left Main Chart

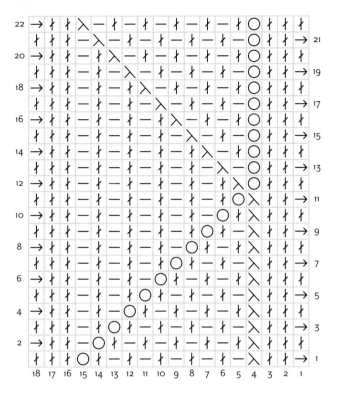

Right Main Chart

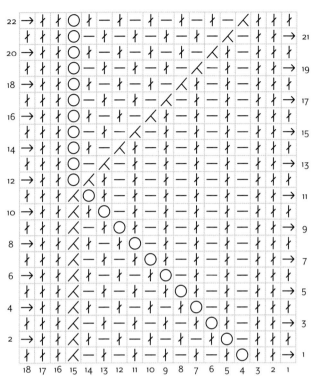

Left End Chart

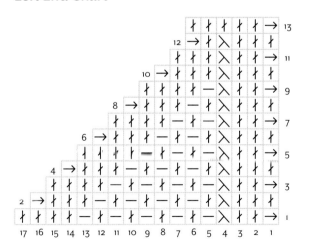

Right End Chart

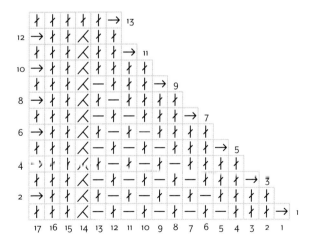

How to Wrap the Strip:

1) The strip starts on the outside of your wrist

2) Wrap the strip around your wrist once. Use a safety pin to carefully mark where the edges first meet.

3) Wrap it around again.

4) Wrap it around once more.

5) Bring it up, across your palm, between your thumb and index finger, and over the back of your hand.

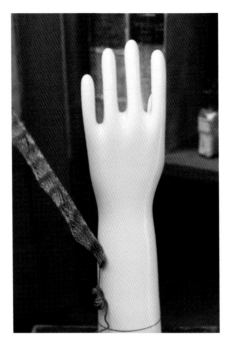
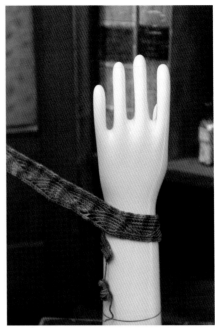
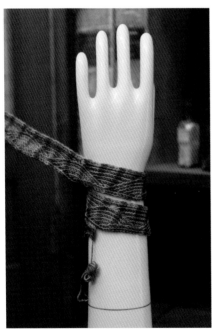
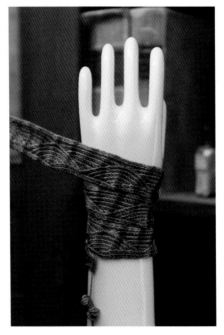
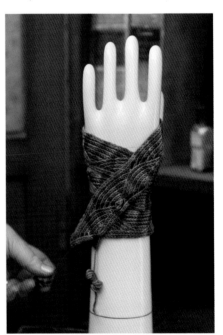

POLYOMMATUS ARGIOLUS

POLYOMMATUS CORYDON

The surface of the male is a very light silvery

blue, with a fine silky lustre, the hinder margin of all the

wings having a blackish band, surmounted in the hinder

pair by a series of dusky, somewhat ocellated spots ...

The underside of both sexes is similar but the secondary

wings in the female are more deeply coloured, and the

spots larger and more distinctly marked; the anterior

wings whitish ... the hinder [ones] of a similar

colour, greenish at the base.

James Duncan

PLATE 32.

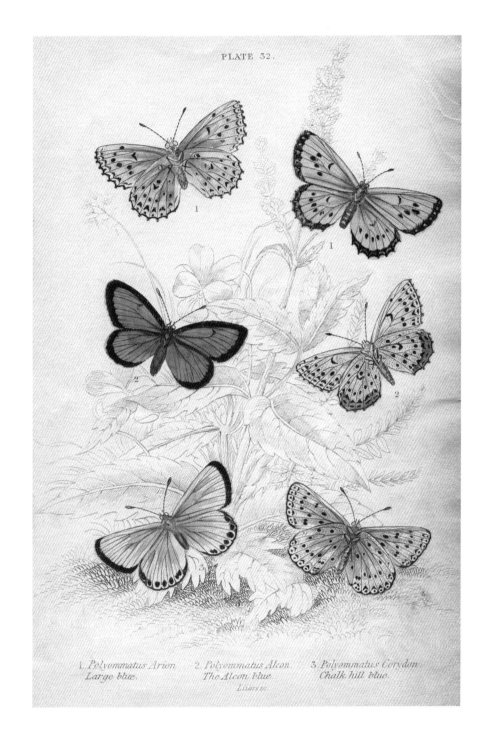

1. *Polyommatus Arion.*
Large blue.

2. *Polyommatus Alcon.*
The Alcon blue.

3. *Polyommatus Corydon.*
Chalk hill blue.

Lizars sc.

POLYOMMATUS CORYDON SOCK

Shown in: Caper Sock by String Theory in the color Blue Hill. Made in size Medium with about 385 yards of yarn.
Gauge and sizing: 8 stitches in 1 inch in stockinette. Fits a foot or leg of about 7.5 [8.5, 9.5, 10.5] inches.
Notes: You will need an extra set of needles to temporarily hold some stitches. Joining the ruffle to the body of the sock can be a bit fiddly. You may find it helpful to safety pin the two pieces together. Consider putting in life lines and double checking that all stitches are correctly joined before moving on to the next part.

Cast on: Cast on 224 [256, 288, 320] stitches. Place marker and join for working in the round.

Ruffles: Work the Ruffle Chart once. 56 [64, 72, 80] stitches remain. Break yarn leaving a tail. Set this piece aside. It is called the first ruffle in the instructions below.

Cast on 224 [256, 288, 320] stitches. Place marker and join for working in the round. Work row 1 and 2 of the Ruffle Chart. 56 [64, 72, 80] stitches remain. This piece is called the second ruffle. Place the second ruffle on top of the first ruffle. Join the ruffles by knitting the next stitch of each ruffle together. That is, put your right needle into the first stitch on the needle holding the second ruffle and into the first stitch on the needle holding the second ruffle, and knit the stitches together. Work 1 round in this fashion. The first and second ruffle are joined (your spare set of needles will now be empty). Work 5 rounds of k. Break yarn leaving a tail. Set this piece aside.

Cast on 224 [256, 288, 320] stitches. Place marker and join for working in the round. Work row 1 and 2 of the Ruffle Chart. 56 [64, 72, 80] stitches remain. This piece is called the third ruffle. Place the third ruffle on top of the second ruffle. Join the ruffles as above. The first, second, and third ruffles are joined (your spare set of needles will now be empty). Work 5 rounds of k. Break yarn leaving a tail. Set this piece aside.

Cast on 224 [256, 288, 320] stitches. Place marker and join for working in the round. Work row 1 and 2 of the Ruffle Chart. 56 [64, 72, 80] stitches remain. This piece is called the fourth ruffle. Place the fourth ruffle on top of the third ruffle. Join the ruffles as above. The first, second, third, and fourth ruffles are joined (your spare set of needles will now be empty). Work 5 rounds of k.

Work 1 round of p.

Turn the cuff. To do this, wrap the yarn around the next stitch by bringing the yarn to the front, slipping the first stitch of the next round to the right hand needle, bringing the yarn to the back, and slipping the same stitch back to the left needle.

Next, turn the cuff inside out (along the purl ridge) so that the inside of the cuff is facing out. This ensures that the outside of the cuff will show when the cuff is turned down when the sock is worn.

Finally, place marker to indicate start of round.

Work 36 rows of p1, k3 ribbing.

Heel flap: The heel flap is worked over stitches 30-56 [34-64, 38-72, 42-80]. It uses 27 [31, 35, 39] stitches.

Row 1 is a wrong-side row (worked with the inside of the sock facing you). Row 2 is a right-side row (worked with the outside of the sock facing you). Work these 2 rows 13 [15, 17, 19] times or until heel flap reaches desired length.

Row 1 (WS): Sl1, p2, (k1, p1, sl1, p1) 5 [6, 7, 8] times, k1, p3.
Row 2 (RS): Sl1, k2, (p1, k3) 6 [7, 8, 9] times.

Heel turn: Odd rows are wrong-side rows (worked with the inside of the sock facing you). Even rows are right-side rows (worked with the outside of the sock facing you). Turn at the end of each row.

Row 1 (WS): Sl1, p15 [17, 19, 21], p2tog, p1.
Row 2 (RS): Sl1, k6, ssk, k1.
Row 3 (WS): Sl1, p7, p2tog, p1.
Row 4 (RS): Sl1, k8, ssk, k1.
Row 5 (WS): Sl1, p9, p2tog, p1.
Row 6 (RS): Sl1, k10, ssk, k1.
Row 7 (WS): Sl1, p11, p2tog, p1.
Row 8 (RS): Sl1, k12, ssk, k1.
Row 9 (WS): Sl1, p13, p2tog, p1.
Row 10 (RS): Sl1, k14, ssk, k1.

Medium, Large and Extra Large, as above plus:
Row 11 (WS): Sl1, p15, p2tog, p1.
Row 12 (RS): Sl1, k16, ssk, k1.

Large and Extra Large, as above plus:
Row 13 (WS): Sl1, p17, p2tog, p1.
Row 14 (RS): Sl1, k18, ssk, k1.

Extra Large, as above plus:
Row 15 (WS): Sl1, p19, p2tog, p1.
Row 16 (RS): Sl1, k20, ssk, k1.

17 [19, 21, 23] stitches remain.

Gusset and foot:
Setup round: Pick up and knit 1 stitch in each of the slipped stitches along the side of the heel flap, place first marker. Work across the top of the foot continuing the p1, k3 ribbing as established, beginning and ending with a p, place second marker. Pick up and knit 1 stitch in each of the slipped stitches along the other side of the heel flap, k8 [9, 10, 11]. The round now begins in the middle of the bottom of the foot.

Decrease round: K until 3 stitches remain before first marker, k2tog, k1. Work across the top of the foot continuing the ribbing as established. K1, ssk, k to end of round. 2 stitches decreased.

Non-decrease round: K to first marker. Work across the top of the foot continuing the ribbing as established. K to end of round.

Alternate decrease and non-decrease rounds until 58 [66, 74, 82] stitches remain. Repeat the non-decrease round until sock measures 2 [2.25, 2.5, 2.75] inches shorter than desired length.

Toe:
Decrease round: K until 3 stitches remain before first marker, k2tog, k1. P1, ssk, follow ribbing as established until 3 stitches remain before second marker, k2tog, p1. K1, ssk, k to end of round. 4 stitches decreased.

Non-decrease round: K to first marker. Follow ribbing as established to second marker. K to end of round.

Work these 2 rounds 4 [6, 8, 10] times, 42 stitches remain. Work the decrease round 6 more times, 18 stitches remain. K to marker. Remove markers. Graft toes. Weave in ends.

Stitch Key

| Knit

/ Right-leaning knit decrease

Slipped decrease

Ruffle Chart

POLYOMMATUS CORYDON HAT

Shown in: Blue Faced Sport by String Theory in the color Grove. Made in size Large with about 200 yards of yarn.

Gauge and sizing: 20 stitches in 4 inches in 2 by 2 ribbing. Fits a head of 17 [20.25, 23.5] inches.

Notes: Shown with the brim cuffed. This is optional, and you can wear either way. Just be sure you make the hat tall enough if you want to wear it with the brim cuffed.

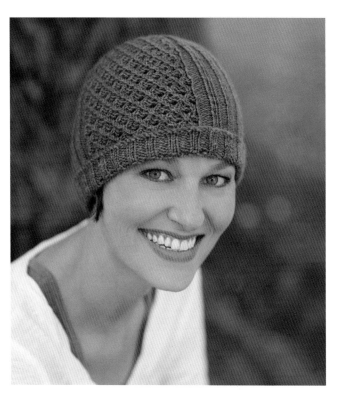

Cast on: Cast on 80 [96, 112] stitches. Place marker (called the end of round marker) and join for working in the round. Place 3 more markers to divide the hat into quarters. These are located after the 20th [24th, 28th] stitch (called the first marker), the 40th [48th, 56th] stitch (called the second marker), and the 60th [72nd, 84th] stitch (called the third marker).

Body: Work row 1 of the Main Chart 8 times. Work rows 2-9 until hat reaches desired height before the decreases. Stop after completing row 9 of the Main Chart.

Decreases: The decreases use two different charts. Follow Decrease Chart A to the first marker. Follow Decrease Chart B to the second marker. Follow Decrease Chart A to the third marker. Follow Decrease Chart B to the end of round marker.

Work through the Decrease Charts in this fashion once. Do not work the final purl stitch at the end of the last round. 16 stitches remain. Remove markers. (Work a left-leaning purl decrease, work a left-leaning twisted knit decrease) 4 times. 8 stitches remain.

Finishing: Draw the yarn through remaining stitches. Weave in ends. Block if desired.

Main Chart

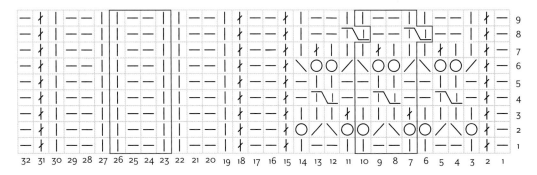

Decrease Chart A

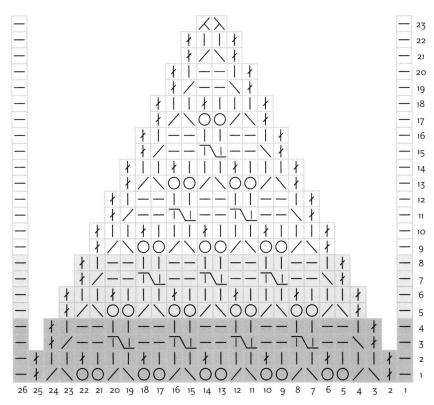

Decrease Chart B

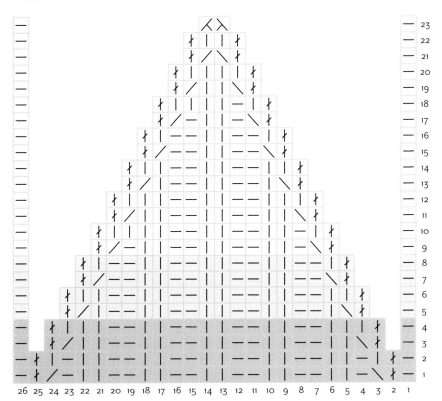

23
22
21
20
19
18
17
16
15
14
13
12
11
10
9
8
7
6
5
4
3
2
1

26 25 24 23 22 21 20 19 18 17 16 15 14 13 12 11 10 9 8 7 6 5 4 3 2 1

Stitch Key

| | Knit

| Knit through the back loop

— Purl

○ Yarn over

/ Right-leaning knit decrease

\ Left-leaning knit decrease

⋋ Right-leaning twisted knit decrease

⋌ Left-leaning twisted knit decrease

1x1 Cable left

☐ Work these stitches 2 [3, 4] times

Work for Medium and Large

Work for Large

Chart Notes: The stitches surrounded by the red border are repeated to adjust the size of the hat. Work them 2 [3, 4] times.

The shaded stitches are used to adjust sizing. On all charts, work only the unshaded stitches for size Small. Work the unshaded stitches and the light gray stitches for size Medium. Work all stitches for size Large.

DELIAS EUCHARIS

This species, which must be well known to everyone
who has seen a case of Butterflies from India, measures
about three inches across the wings ... The marginal area
is marked off by a transverse black line, outside which is
a series of large oval spots, separated by the nervures.
On the fore-wings these are of the ground-colour
in the male, but tinged with yellow towards the
tip in the female.

William Forsell Kirby

PLATE LVI.

3.

1.

2.

Wyman & Sons Limited.

1. 2. *Delias eucharis.*
3.   „   *philyra.*

DELIAS EUCHARIS SOCK

Shown in: Plucky Feet by Plucky Knitter in the color Sticky Toffee.
Made in size Medium with about 375 yards of yarn.
Gauge and sizing: 8 stitches in 1 inch in stockinette. Fits a foot or leg of about 7.5 [8.5, 9.5] inches.

Cast on: Cast on 62 [70, 78] stitches. Place marker and join for working in the round.

Cuff and leg: Work the Main Chart until sock reaches desired height. Stop after completing row 8 of the Main Chart.

Heel flap: The heel flap is worked over stitches 31-62 [35-70, 39-78]. It uses 32 [36, 40] stitches.

Odd rows are wrong-side rows (worked with the inside of the sock facing you, following the wrong-side notations in the stitch key, and reading the chart from left to right). Even rows are right-side rows (worked with the outside of the sock facing you, following the right-side notations in the stitch key, and reading the chart from right to left). Work the Heel Chart 8 [9, 10] times or until heel flap reaches desired length.

Heel turn: Odd rows are wrong-side rows (worked with the inside of the sock facing you). Even rows are right-side rows (worked with the outside of the sock facing you). Turn at the end of each row.

Row 1 (WS): Sl1, p18 [20, 22], p2tog, p1.
Row 2 (RS): Sl1, k7, ssk, k1.
Row 3 (WS): Sl1, p8, p2tog, p1.
Row 4 (RS): Sl1, k9, ssk, k1.
Row 5 (WS): Sl1, p10, p2tog, p1.
Row 6 (RS): Sl1, k11, ssk, k1.
Row 7 (WS): Sl1, p12, p2tog, p1.
Row 8 (RS): Sl1, k13, ssk, k1.

Row 9 (WS): Sl1, p14, p2tog, p1.
Row 10 (RS): Sl1, k15, ssk, k1.
Row 11 (WS): Sl1, p16, p2tog, p1.
Row 12 (RS): Sl1, k17, ssk, k1.

For Medium and Large, as above plus:
Row 13 (WS): Sl1, p18, p2tog, p1.
Row 14 (RS): Sl1, k19, ssk, k1.

For Large, as above plus:
Row 15 (WS): Sl1, p20, p2tog, p1.
Row 16 (RS): Sl1, k21, ssk, k1.

20 [22, 24] stitches remain.

Gusset and foot:
Setup round: Pick up and knit stitches along the side of the heel flap, place first marker. Work across the top of the foot following 30 [34, 38] stitches of the first row of the Main Chart (you are no longer working stitch 35 [37, 39] of the Main Chart), place second marker. Pick up and knit stitches along the other side of the heel flap, k10 [11, 12]. The round now begins in the middle of the bottom of the foot.

Decrease round: K until 3 stitches remain before first marker, k2tog, p1. Work across the top of the foot following 30 [34, 38] stitches of the next row of the Main Chart (you are no longer working stitch 35 [37, 39] of the Main Chart). P1, ssk, k to end of round. 2 stitches decreased.

Non-decrease round: K until 1 stitch remain before first marker, p1. Work across the top of the foot following 30 [34, 38] stitches of the next row of the Main Chart (you are no longer working stitch 35 [37, 39] of the Main Chart). P1, k to end of round.

Alternate decrease and non-decrease rounds until 60 [68, 76] stitches remain. Repeat the non-decrease round until sock measures 2 [2.25, 2.5] inches shorter than desired length. Stop after completing row 4 or row 8 of the Main Chart. Repeat row 1 of the Main Chart as needed to adjust length.

Toe:
Decrease round: K until 3 stitches remain before first marker, k2tog, p1. Ktbl1, p1, work a left-leaning twisted decrease, follow ribbing as established by row 1 of the Main Chart until 4 stitches remain before second marker, work a right-leaning twisted decrease, p1, ktbl1. P1, ssk, k to end of round. 4 stitches decreased.

Non-decrease round: K until 1 stitch remains before first marker, p1. Follow ribbing as established by row 1 of the Main Chart to second marker. P1, k to end of round.

Work these 2 rounds 4 [6, 8] times, 44 stitches remain. Work the decrease round 6 more times, 20 stitches remain. K to marker. Remove markers. Graft toes. Weave in ends.

Stitch Key

	RS: Knit WS: Purl
	RS: Knit through the back loop WS: Purl through the back loop
	RS: Purl WS: Knit
	Yarn over
	Slip as if to purl
	Right-leaning knit decrease
	Left-leaning knit decrease
	1x2x1 Cable right
	1x2x1 Cable left
	Work for Medium and Large
	Work for Large

Main Chart

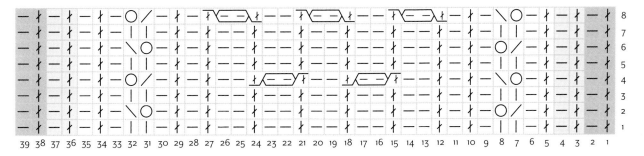

Heel Chart

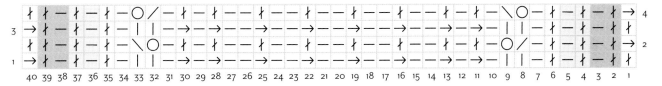

Chart notes: The shaded stitches are used to adjust sizing. On all charts, work only the unshaded stitches for size Small. Work the unshaded stitches and the light gray stitches for size Medium. Work all stitches for size Large.

DELIAS EUCHARIS HAT

Shown in: Primo MCN Worsted by Plucky Knitter in the color Flying Monkey. Made in size Medium with about 175 yards of yarn.
Gauge and sizing: 12 stitches in 2 inches in ribbing as shown on first 4 rows of Brim Chart. Fits a head of 19 [21, 23, 25] inches.
Notes: The decreases happen very quickly (in just 6 rounds). You won't get any extra height from them. Be sure the hat is as tall as you'd like it to be before you begin working the decreases.

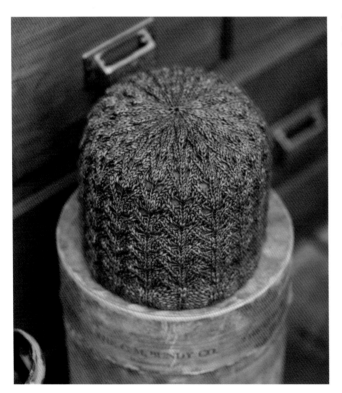

Cast on: Cast on 108 [120, 132, 144] stitches. Place marker and join for working in the round.

Brim: Work the Brim Chart once. Stop after completing row 12 of the Brim Chart.

Body: Work the Main Chart until hat reaches desired height before the decreases. Stop after completing row 8 of the Main Chart.

Decreases: Work the Decrease Chart once. 9 [10, 11, 12] stitches remain.

Finishing: Draw the yarn through remaining stitches. Weave in ends. Block if desired.

Stitch Key

| | Knit

— Purl

◯ Yarn over

╱ Right-leaning knit decrease

╲ Left-leaning knit decrease

Brim Chart

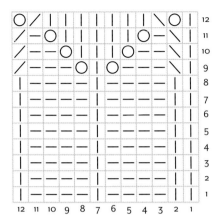

Main Chart

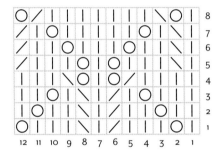

Decrease Chart

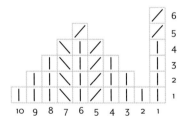

ERASMIA PULCHELLA

This Moth ... was first brought from Assam, but is likewise found in most of the adjoining countries of Northern India. The prevailing colour is silvery-green; the fore-wings are black, ornamented with greenish-blue silvery spots; there is an irregular orange-red band before the middle, separated by a bluish-green band from a series of large white spots beyond the middle; the hind-wings are straw-coloured, black at the base, and with a black border.

William Forsell Kirby

PLATE LXXVIII.

Wyman & Sons Limited.

1. *Devanica tricolor.*
2. *Erasmia pulchella.*
3. *Amesia sanguiflua.*

ERASMIA PULCHELLA SOCK

Shown in: Sock by Shibui in the color Wasabi. Made in size Medium with about 350 yards of yarn.
Gauge and sizing: 8 stitches in 1 inch in stockinette. Fits a foot or leg of about 7.5 [8.5, 9.5, 10.5] inches.

Cast on: Cast on 56 [64, 72, 80] stitches. Place marker and join for working in the round.

Cuff and leg: Work the Cuff Chart 8 times. Work the appropriate Chart A until sock reaches desired height. Stop after completing row 2 of the appropriate Chart A.

Heel flap: The heel flap is worked over stitches 30-56 [34-64, 38-72, 42-80]. It uses a total of 27 [31, 35, 39] stitches.

Row 1 is a wrong-side row (worked with the inside of the sock facing you). Row 2 is a right-side row (worked with the outside of the sock facing you). Work these 2 rows 13 [15, 17, 19] times or until heel flap reaches desired length.

Row 1 (WS): Sl1, p2, (k1, p3) 6 [7, 8, 9] times.
Row 2 (RS): Sl1, k2, (p1, k3) 6 [7, 8, 9] times.

Heel turn: Odd rows are wrong-side rows (worked with the inside of the sock facing you). Even rows are right-side rows (worked with the outside of the sock facing you). Turn at the end of each row.

Row 1 (WS): Sl1, p15 [17, 19, 21], p2tog, p1.
Row 2 (RS): Sl1, k6, ssk, k1.
Row 3 (WS): Sl1, p7, p2tog, p1.
Row 4 (RS): Sl1, k8, ssk, k1.

Row 5 (WS): Sl1, p9, p2tog, p1.
Row 6 (RS): Sl1, k10, ssk, k1.
Row 7 (WS): Sl1, p11, p2tog, p1.
Row 8 (RS): Sl1, k12, ssk, k1.
Row 9 (WS): Sl1, p13, p2tog, p1.
Row 10 (RS): Sl1, k14, ssk, k1.

For Medium, Large, and Extra Large, as above plus:
Row 11 (WS): Sl1, p15, p2tog, p1.
Row 12 (RS): Sl1, k16, ssk, k1.

For Large and Extra Large, as above plus:
Row 13 (WS): Sl1, p17, p2tog, p1.
Row 14 (RS): Sl1, k18, ssk, k1.

For Extra Large, as above plus:
Row 15 (WS): Sl1, p19, p2tog, p1.
Row 16 (RS): Sl1, k20, ssk, k1.

17 [19, 21, 23] stitches remain.

Gusset and foot: Charts A and B alternate on the foot. Start by working Chart A once, then Chart B once. Then work Chart A once and Chart B twice. Then work Chart A once and Chart B 3 times. Continue in this fashion, working Chart B an additional time each cycle, as you make your way down the foot.

Setup round: Pick up and knit 1 stitch in each of the slipped stitches along the side of the heel flap, place first marker. Work across the top of the foot following the first row of the appropriate Chart A You will work 3 [4, 4, 5] full repeats of Chart A and 5 [1, 5, 1] stitches from another repeat of Chart A (when counting stitches, the yarn over cluster represents 3 stitches). Place second marker. Pick up and knit 1 stitch in each of the slipped stitches along the other side of the heel flap, k8 [9, 10, 11]. The round now begins in the middle of the bottom of the foot.

Decrease round: K until 3 stitches remain before first marker, k2tog, k1. Work across the top of the foot following the next row of the appropriate Chart (you will work 3 [4, 4, 5] full repeats of the chart and 5 [1, 5, 1] stitches from another repeat of the chart). K1, ssk, k to end of round. 2 stitches decreased.

Non-decrease round: K to first marker. Work across the top of the foot following the next row of the appropriate Chart (you will work 3 [4, 4, 5] full repeats of the chart and 5 [1, 5, 1] stitches from another repeat of the chart). K to end of round.

Alternate decrease and non-decrease rounds until 58 [66, 74, 82] stitches remain. Repeat the non-decrease round until sock measures 2 [2.25, 2.5, 2.75] inches shorter than desired length. Stop after completing row 1 of the appropriate chart.

Toe:
Decrease round: K until 3 stitches remain before first marker, k2tog, k1. P1, ssk, follow ribbing as established by the appropriate Chart B until 3 stitches remain before second marker, k2tog, p1. K1, ssk, k to end of round. 4 stitches decreased.

Non-decrease round: K to first marker. Follow ribbing as established by the appropriate Chart B to second marker. K to end of round. 4 stitches decreased.

Work these 2 rounds 4 [6, 8, 10] times, 42 stitches remain. Work the decrease round 7 more times, 14 stitches remain. K to first marker. Remove markers. Graft toes. Weave in ends.

Stitch Key

| | Knit

⅄ Knit through the back loop

— Purl

→ Slip as if to purl

| | | | ◯ Yarn over cluster

No stitch

Cuff Chart

Left Chart A

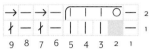

Left Chart B

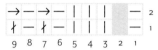

Right Chart A

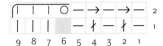

Right Chart B

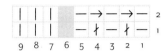

Chart notes: The left and right socks use different charts. Be sure to follow the appropriate charts.

Charts A and B alternate in a particular way on the foot. Pay close attention to the instructions.

ERASMIA PULCHELLA HAT

Shown in: Baby Alpaca by Shibui in the color Flaxen. Made in size Medium with about 175 yards of yarn.
Gauge and sizing: 22 stitches in 3 inches in stockinette. Fits a head of 19 [22, 25] inches.

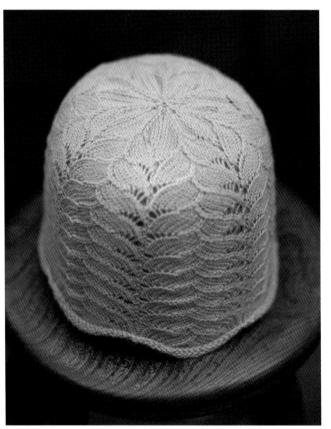

Cast on: Cast on 132 [154, 176] stitches. Place marker and join for working in the round.

Brim: Work the Brim Chart once.

Body: Work the Main Chart until hat reaches desired height. The height will depend on how slouchy you want the hat to be. The hat shown is about 7 inches high before the decreases. Stop after completing row 6 of the Main Chart.

Decreases: Work the Decrease Chart once. 12 [14, 16] stitches remain.

Finishing: Draw the yarn through remaining stitches. Weave in ends. Block if desired.

Stitch Key

| | Knit

ł Knit through the back loop

— Purl

→ Slip as if to purl

◯ Yarn over

ⵢ Right-leaning twisted knit decrease

ⵣ Left-leaning twisted knit decrease

Brim Chart

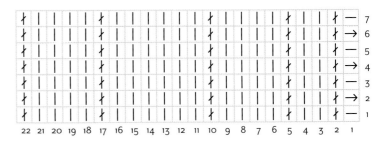

Main Chart

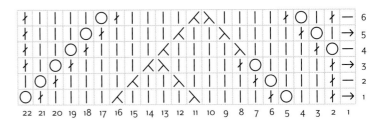

Decrease Chart

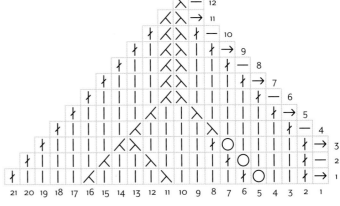

DANIMA BANKSIAE

This Moth is found in Australia and Tasmania ...
In the female the fore-wings are of a leaden colour,
glossed with purple, with a few black marks, and freckled
here and there with white and orange-coloured dots, and
also several clouds and dashes of the same colour. The
fringes are brown. The hind-wings are uniform glossy-
brown with lighter fringes.

William Forsell Kirby

PLATE XCV.

DANIMA BANKSIAE

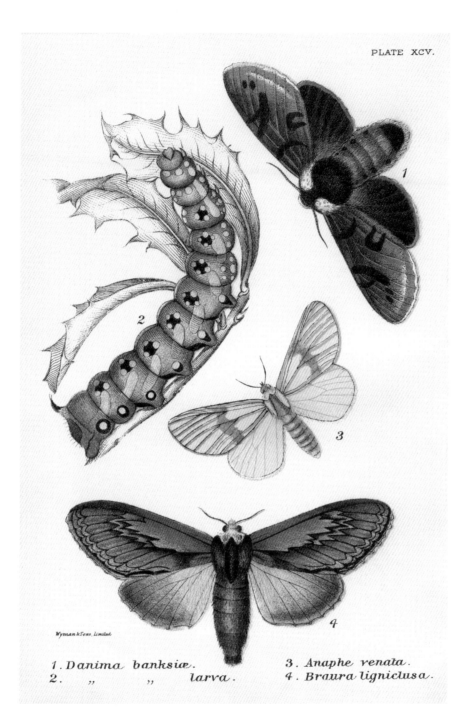

1. Danima banksiæ.
2.   „   „   larva.
3. Anaphe renata.
4. Braura ligniclusa.

Wyman&Sons, Limited.

DANIMA BANKSIAE SOCK

Shown in: Pali by Saffron Dyeworks in the color Blue Greyonyx. Made in size Medium with about 350 yards of yarn.
Gauge and sizing: 6 stitches in 1 inch in Main Chart pattern. Fits a foot or leg of about 7.5 [8.5, 9.5, 10.5] inches.
Notes: The lace fabric is quite open and so requires fewer stitches to produce a given width of fabric. This explains the low stitch count in the leg. To ensure a good fit, there are some adjustments made in the gusset. Pay close attention to the instructions.

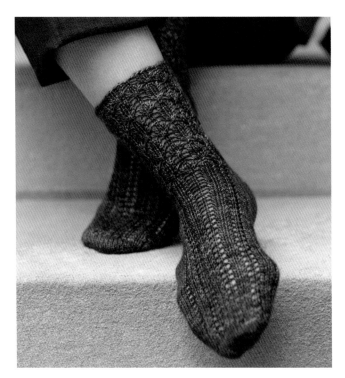

Cast on: Cast on 56 [64, 72, 80] stitches. Place marker and join for working in the round.

Cuff and leg: Work the Cuff Chart once. 42 [48, 54, 60] stitches remain. Work the Main Chart until sock reaches desired height. Stop after completing row 12 of the Main Chart.

Heel flap: For the Small and Large sizes only, you must shift your start of round marker back 1 stitch before you work the heel flap. To do this, the last time you work row 12 of the Main Chart, do not work the very last stitch of the round. That stitch (42 or 54 depending on the size you're making) is now the first stitch of your round. Shift your stitch marker to indicate this before you identify the stitches for your heel flap.

The heel flap is worked over stitches 22-42 [26-48, 28-54, 32-60]. It uses 21 [23, 27, 29] stitches.

Row 1 is a wrong-side row (worked with the inside of the sock facing you, following the wrong-side notations in the stitch key, and reading the chart from left to right). Row 2 is a right-side row (worked with the outside of the sock facing you, following the right-side notations in

the stitch key, and reading the chart from right to left). Work the Heel Chart 14 [16, 18, 20] times or until heel flap reaches desired length.

Heel turn: Odd rows are wrong-side rows (worked with the inside of the sock facing you). Even rows are right-side rows (worked with the outside of the sock facing you). Turn at the end of each row.

Row 1 (WS): Sl1, p11 [13, 15, 15], p2tog, p1.
Row 2 (RS): Sl1, k4 [6, 6, 4], ssk, k1.
Row 3 (WS): Sl1, p5 [7, 7, 5], p2tog, p1.
Row 4 (RS): Sl1, k6 [8, 8, 6], ssk, k1.
Row 5 (WS): Sl1, p7 [9, 9, 7], p2tog, p1.
Row 6 (RS): Sl1, k8 [10, 10, 8], ssk, k1.
Row 7 (WS): Sl1, p9 [11, 11, 9], p2tog, p1.
Row 8 (RS): Sl1, k10 [12, 12, 10], ssk, k1.

For Large and Extra Large, as above plus:
Row 9 (WS): Sl1, p— [—, 13, 11], p2tog, p1.
Row 10 (RS): Sl1, k— [—, 14, 12], ssk, k1.

For Extra Large, as above plus:
Row 11 (WS): Sl1, p— [—, —, 13], p2tog, p1.
Row 12 (RS): Sl1, k— [—, —, 14], ssk, k1.

13 [15, 17, 17] stitches remain.

Gusset and foot:
Setup round: Pick up and knit stitches along the side of the heel flap, place first marker. Work across the top of the foot following the first row of the appropriate Foot Chart, place second marker. Pick up and knit stitches along the other side of the heel flap, k7 [8, 9, 9]. The round now begins in the middle of the bottom of the foot.

Decrease round: K until 3 stitches remain before first marker, k2tog, k1. Work across the top of the foot following the next row of the appropriate Foot Chart. K1, ssk, k to end of round. 2 stitches decreased.

Non-decrease round: K to first marker. Work across the top of the foot following the next row of the appropriate Foot Chart. K to end of round.

Alternate decrease and non-decrease rounds until 48 [56, 60, 68] stitches remain. The bottom of the foot will have 6 stitches more than the top of the foot. Repeat the non-decrease round until sock measures 1.75 [2, 2.25, 2.5] inches shorter than desired length. Stop after completing row 2 of the appropriate Foot Chart.

Toe:
Initial decrease round: K until 3 stitches remain before first marker, k2tog, k1. Work across the top of the foot following the appropriate Foot Chart. K1, ssk, k to end of round. 2 stitches decreased.

Initial non-decrease round: K to first marker. Work across the top of the foot following the appropriate Foot Chart. K to end of round.

Work these 2 rounds 3 times, 42 [50, 54, 62] stitches remain.

Decrease round: K until 3 stitches remain before first marker, k2tog, k1. K1, ssk, k until 3 stitches remain before second marker, k2tog, k1. K1, ssk, k to end of round. 4 stitches decreased.

Non-decrease round: K to end of round.

Work these 2 rounds 0 [2, 3, 5] times, 42 stitches remain. Work the decrease round 6 more times, 18 stitches remain. K to first marker. Remove markers. Graft toes. Weave in ends.

Cuff Chart

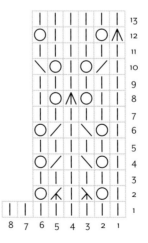

Main Chart

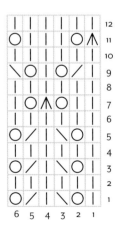

Stitch Key

| RS: Knit
WS: Purl

— RS: Purl
WS: Knit

→ Slip as if to purl

O Yarn over

╱ Right-leaning knit decrease

╲ Left-leaning knit decrease

⋏ Right-leaning double knit decrease

⋌ Left-leaning double knit decrease

⋏ Centered double knit decrease

☐ Work these stitches 2 [2, 3, 3] times

Chart notes: The sizes use different Heel and Foot charts. Be sure to follow the appropriate charts.

Stitches surrounded by a red border are repeated to adjust the size of the sock. Work them 2 [2, 3, 3] times.

When a centered double decrease is the first stitch on the needle, it requires extra attention. The double decrease turns 3 stitches into 1. When it happens at the beginning of a needle, the first of those 3 stitches is the last stitch of the previous needle.

For example, the first stitch of round 12 of the Cuff Chart is a centered double decrease. The decrease will use the last stitch of round 11 and the first 2 stitches of round 12. To make the decrease, do not work the last stitch of round 11. Instead, use it as the first of the 3 stitches of the decrease as described in the stitch key. The completed stitch will be the first stitch of round 12.

Heel Chart (Small and Large)

Heel Chart (Medium and Extra Large)

Foot Chart (Small and Large)

Foot Chart (Medium and Extra Large)

DANIMA BANKSIAE MITT

Shown in: Mica by Saffron Dyeworks in the color Ginger Snap. Made in size Small with about 125 yards of yarn.
Gauge and sizing: 6 stitches in 1 inch in ribbing as shown in the Main Chart. Fits an arm of about 6 [8] inches. Measure at the widest part of the arm that you want the mitt to cover.

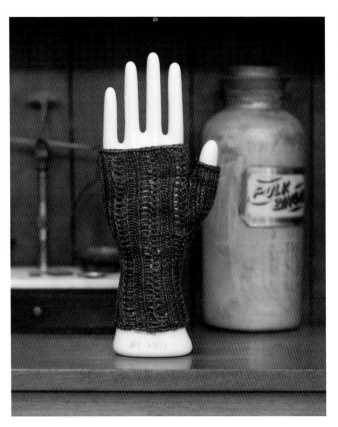

Cast on: Cast on 36 [48] stitches. Place marker and join for working in the round.

Wrist: Work the Setup Chart once. Work it as follows. Work columns 1-6 3 [4] times, then work columns 7-12 3 [4] times.

Work the Main Chart until the wrist reaches desired length (measured to the base of the palm). Work it as follows. Work columns 1-6 3 [4] times, then work columns 7-12 3 [4] times. Stop after completing row 2 of the Main Chart.

Thumb: To make the thumb gusset, you will gradually create 12 extra stitches.

Left thumb gusset: Locate the first stitch of the round. Place a stitch marker on each side of this stitch. Work the next row of the Thumb Chart over the stitches between these stitch markers. Work the rest of the round in ribbing as established. Work through the Thumb Charts in this fashion once. You will have a total of 48 [60] stitches.

Right thumb gusset: Locate the 19th [25th] stitch of the round. Place a stitch marker on each side of this stitch. Work to the first of these stitch markers in ribbing as established. Work the next row of the Thumb Chart over the stitches between these stitch markers. Work the rest of the round in ribbing as established. Work through the

Thumb Charts in this fashion once. You will have a total of 48 [60] stitches.

Hand, part 1. Work in ribbing as established for 10 [12] rounds.

Hand, part 2: You will now set aside the stitches for the thumb gusset (the 12 stitches you created and the central purl stitch 'borrowed' at the base of the gusset).

Left hand: Locate and set aside stitches 1-13 on a spare needle or length of scrap yarn. Remove the stitch markers used to mark off the thumb stitches. Cast on 1 stitch (to make up for the central purl stitch you 'borrowed' at the base of the gusset). You will have a total of 36 [48] stitches on your active needles and 13 stitches on a spare needle. Work in ribbing as established for 11 rounds. Work the Final Chart once. Cast off loosely.

Right hand: Locate and set aside stitches 19-31 [25-37] on a spare needle or length of scrap yarn. Remove the stitch markers used to mark off the thumb stitches. Work in ribbing as established to thumb stitches. Cast on 1 stitch (to make up for the central purl stitch you 'borrowed' at the base of the gusset).Work to end of round in ribbing as established. You will have a total of 36 [48] stitches on your active needles and 13 stitches on a spare needle. Work in ribbing as established for 10 rounds. Work the Final Chart once. Cast off loosely.

Thumb: Divide the 13 stitches set aside for the thumb across two needles. Pick up 5 stitches to bridge the gap between the first and last of the set aside thumb stitches. You will have 18 thumb stitches. Work in ribbing as shown in the Final Chart for 6 rounds.

Finishing: Cast off loosely. Weave in ends. Block if desired.

Chart Notes: The charts are read in a sightly unusual way. Pay close attention to the instructions.

One of the stitches in the chart tells you to knit, wrapping the yarn around the needle twice. When you come to this stitch in the next round, drop the extra loop of yarn off your needle.

Stitch Key

| | | Knit

| ⅄ | Knit through the back loop

| OO | Knit wrapping the yarn twice

| — | Purl

| Ϝ | Make 1 right knitwise

| Ƚ | Make 1 right purlwise

| Ɏ | Make 1 left knitwise

| Ⴤ | Make 1 left purwise

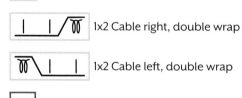 1x2 Cable right, double wrap

1x2 Cable left, double wrap

| | Work these stitches 3 [4] times

Setup Chart

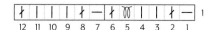

Main Chart

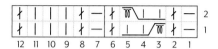

Thumb Chart

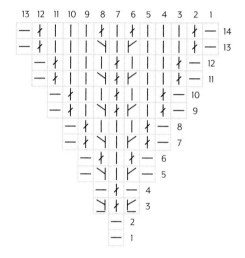

Final Chart

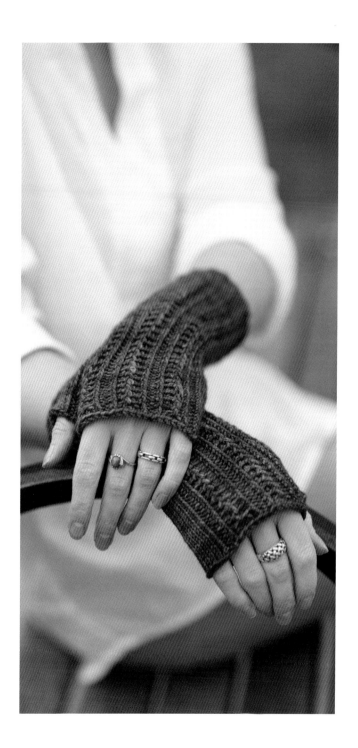

SMERINTHUS OCELLATUS

The Eyed Hawk-moth is found throughout Europe,

and Northern and Western Asia ... The fore-wings, which

are very pointed at the tips, are gray tinged with rose-colour,

and variegated with brown and dusky clouds and waved

streaks. The center is marked with a pale, curved, transverse

streak. The hind wings are carmine red, with the costa

entirely gray, and the hind margin tinged with gray.

William Forsell Kirby

PLATE CX.

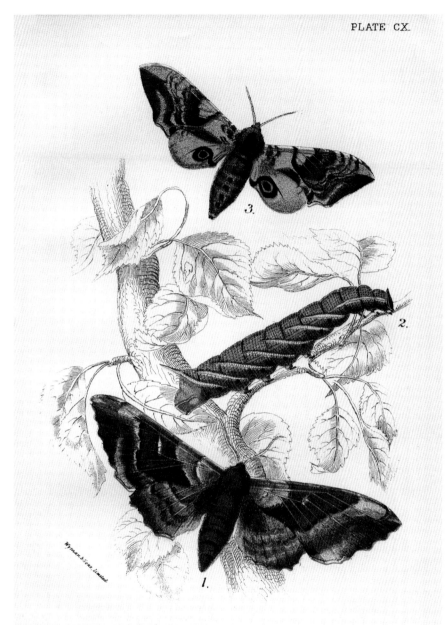

1. *Amorpha populi.*
2.   do.   do, *larva.*
3. *Smerinthus ocellatus*

SMERINTHUS OCELLATUS SOCK

Shown in: Achilles by Barking Dog Yarns in the color Chestnuts on the Flame. Made in size Medium with about 350 yards of yarn.
Gauge and sizing: 8 stitches in 1 inch in stockinette. Fits a foot or leg of about 7.5 [8.5, 9.5, 10.5] inches.
Notes: The heel flap, gusset, foot, and toe directions are different for different sizes. Be sure to follow the appropriate directions.

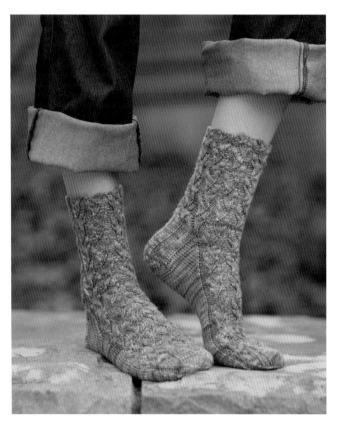

Cast on: Cast on 56 [64, 72, 80] stitches. Place marker and join for working in the round.

Cuff and leg: Work the appropriate Main Chart until sock reaches desired height. Stop after completing row 16 of the appropriate Main Chart.

Heel flap: For the Small and Large sizes only, you must shift your start of round marker back 1 stitch before you work the heel flap. To do this, the last time you work row 16 of the appropriate Main Chart, do not work the very last stitch of the round. That stitch (56 or 72 depending on the size you're making) is now the first stitch of your round. Shift your stitch marker to indicate this before you identify the stitches for your heel flap.

The heel flap is worked over stitches 27-56 [33-64, 35-72, 41-80]. It uses a total of 30 [32, 38, 40] stitches.

Row 1 is a wrong-side row (worked with the inside of the sock facing you). Row 2 is a right-side row (worked with the outside of the sock facing you). Work these 2 rows 13 [15, 17, 19] times or until heel flap reaches desired length.

Small and Large:
Row 1 (WS): Sl1, p1, sl2, p1, ptbl1, k1, (k1, ptbl1, p1, sl2, p1, ptbl1, k1) 2 [3 times], k1, ptbl1, p1, sl2, p2.
Row 2 (RS): Sl1, k4, ktbl1, p1, (p1, ktbl1, k4, ktbl1, p1), 2 [3 times], p1, ktbl1, k5.

Medium and Extra Large:
Row 1 (WS): Sl1, ptbl1, p1, sl2, p1, ptbl1, k1, (k1, ptbl1, p1, sl2, p1, ptbl1, k1) 2 [3 times], k1, ptbl1, p1, sl2, p1, ptbl1, p1.
Row 2 (RS): Sl1, ktbl1, k4, ktbl1, p1, (p1, ktbl1, k4, ktbl1, p1), 2 [3 times], p1, ktbl1, k4, ktbl1, k1.

Heel turn: Odd rows are wrong-side rows (worked with the inside of the sock facing you). Even rows are right-side rows (worked with the outside of the sock facing you). Turn at the end of each row.

Row 1 (WS): Sl1, p16 [18, 20, 22], p2tog, p1.
Row 2 (RS): Sl1, k5 [7, 5, 7], ssk, k1.
Row 3 (WS): Sl1, p6 [8, 6, 8], p2tog, p1.
Row 4 (RS): Sl1, k7 [9, 7, 9], ssk, k1.
Row 5 (WS): Sl1, p8 [10, 8, 10], p2tog, p1.
Row 6 (RS): Sl1, k9 [11, 9, 11], ssk, k1.
Row 7 (WS): Sl1, p10 [12, 10, 12], p2tog, p1.
Row 8 (RS): Sl1, k11 [13, 11, 13], ssk, k1.
Row 9 (WS): Sl1, p12 [14, 12, 14], p2tog, p1.
Row 10 (RS): Sl1, k13 [15, 13, 15], ssk, k1.
Row 11 (WS): Sl1, k14 [16, 14, 16], p2tog, p1.
Row 12 (RS): Sl1, p15 [17, 15, 17], ssk, k1.

For Large and Extra Large, as above plus:
Row 13 (WS): Sl1, p— [—, 16, 18], p2tog, p1.
Row 14 (RS): Sl1, k— [—, 17, 19], ssk, k1.
Row 15 (WS): Sl1, p— [—, 18, 20], p2tog, p1.
Row 16 (RS): Sl1, k— [—, 19, 21], ssk, k1.

18 [20, 22, 24] stitches remain.

Gusset and foot:
Setup round: For the Small and Large sizes, pick up and knit 1 stitch in each of the slipped stitches along the side of the heel flap, place first marker. P1, work across the top of the foot following the first row of the appropriate Main Chart (you will work 3 [4] full repeats of the Main Chart), p1, place second marker. Pick up and knit 1 stitch in each of the slipped stitches along the other side of the heel flap, k9 [11]. The round now begins in the middle of the bottom of the foot.

For the Medium and Extra Large sizes, pick up and knit 1 stitch in each of the slipped stitches along the side of the heel flap, place first marker. Work across the top of the foot following the first row of the appropriate Main Chart (you will work 4 [5] full repeats of the Main Chart), place second marker. Pick up and knit 1 stitch in each of the slipped stitches along the other side of the heel flap, k10 [12]. The round now begins in the middle of the bottom of the foot.

Decrease round: For the Small and Large sizes, k until 3 stitches remain before first marker, k2tog, k1. P1, work across the top of the foot following the next row of the appropriate Main Chart (you will work 3 [4] full repeats of the Main Chart), p1. K1, ssk, k to end of round. 2 stitches decreased.

For the Medium and Extra Large sizes, k until 3 stitches remain before first marker, k2tog, p1. Work across the top of the foot following the next row of the appropriate Main Chart (you will work 4 [5] full repeats of the Main Chart). P1, ssk, k to end of round. 2 stitches decreased.

Non-decrease round: For the Small and Large sizes, k to first marker. P1, work across the top of the foot following the next row of the appropriate Main Chart (you will work 3 [4] full repeats of the Main Chart), p1. K to end of round.

For the Medium and Extra Large sizes, k until 1 stitch remain before first marker, p1. Work across the top of the foot following the next row of the appropriate Main Chart (you will work 4 [5] full repeats of the Main Chart). P1, k to end of round.

Alternate decrease and non-decrease rounds until 52 [64, 68, 80] stitches remain. Repeat the non-decrease round until sock measures 1.75 [2.25, 2.25, 2.75] inches shorter than desired length. Stop after completing row 8 or 16 of the appropriate Main Chart. Repeat row 8 or 16 of the appropriate Main Chart as needed to adjust length.

Toe:
Decrease round: For the Small and Large sizes, k until 3 stitches remain before first marker, k2tog, k1. P2, ssk, follow ribbing as established by row 8 or 16 of the appropriate Main Chart until 4 stitches

remain before second marker, k2tog, p2. K1, ssk, k to end of round. 4 stitches decreased.

For the Medium and Extra Large sizes, k until 3 stitches remain before first marker, k2tog, p1. P1, ssk, follow ribbing as established by row 8 or 16 of the appropriate Main Chart until 3 stitches remain before second marker, k2tog, p1. P1, ssk, k to end of round. 4 stitches decreased.

Non-decrease round: For the Small and Large sizes, k to first marker. Follow ribbing as established by row 8 or 16 of the appropriate Main Chart to second marker. K to end of round.

For the Medium and Extra Large sizes, k until 1 stitch remains before first marker, p1. Follow ribbing as established by row 8 or 16 of the appropriate Main Chart to second marker. P1, k to end of round.

Work these 2 rounds 2 [5, 6, 9] times, 44 stitches remain. Work the decrease round 7 more times, 16 stitches remain. K to first marker. Remove markers. Graft toes. Weave in ends.

Stitch Key

| Knit

⸔ Knit through the back loop

— Purl

◯ Yarn over

⟋ Right-leaning twisted knit decrease

⟍ Left-leaning twisted knit decrease

2x2 Cable right

2x2 Cable left

Left Main Chart

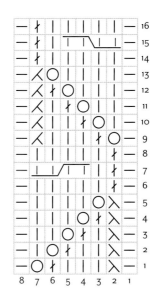

Right Main Chart

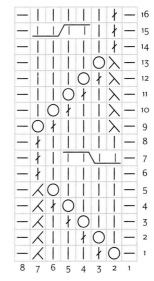

Chart notes: The left and right socks use different charts. Be sure to follow the appropriate charts.

SMERINTHUS OCELLATUS CUFF

Shown in: Galaxy by Barking Dog Yarns in the color Japanese Cherry. Made in size Medium with about 150 yards of yarn.

Gauge and sizing: 14 stitches in 2 inches in stockinette. Fits an arm of about 4.5 [6.75, 9] inches. Measure at the widest part of the arm that you want the cuff to cover.

Cast on: Cast on 28 [42, 56] stitches. Place marker and join for working in the round.

Hand and wrist: Work rows 1-4 of the Main Chart until wrist reaches desired length (measured to the base of the palm). Work rows 5-32 of the Main Chart once. 68 [102, 136] stitches remain.

Finishing: Cast off loosely. Weave in ends. Block if desired.

Main Chart

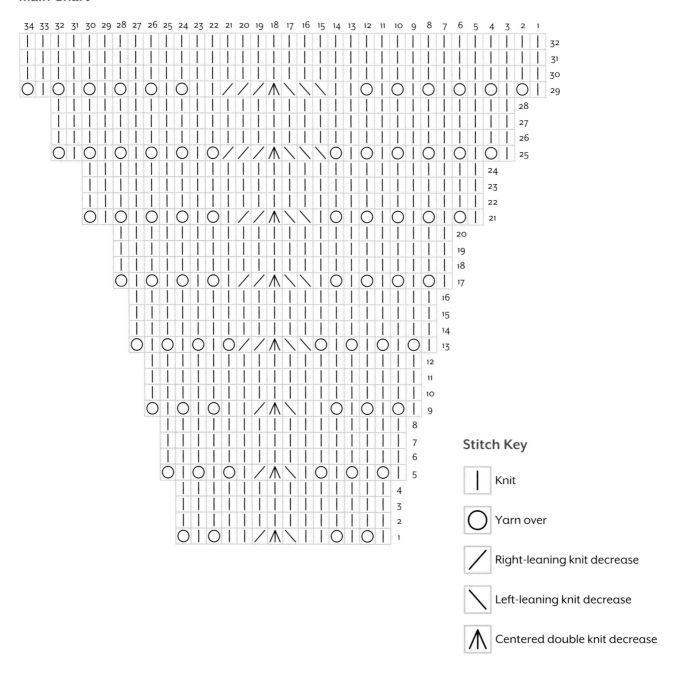

Stitch Key

| | Knit

O Yarn over

/ Right-leaning knit decrease

\ Left-leaning knit decrease

∧ Centered double knit decrease

METOPSILUS PORCELLUS

The Small Elephant Hawk-Moth ... is dull greenish-yellow, with broad rose-coloured hind margins, and a rose-coloured body. The fore-wings have a broad rose-coloured transverse band in front of the middle, and three spots of the same colour on the costa, expanding to the apex. The fringes are also rosy. The hind-wings are blackish towards the base and costa, with white fringes and rosy nervures.

William Forsell Kirby

PLATE XCVIII.

Wyman & Sons Limited.

1. *Chœrocampa elpenor.*
2. *Metopsilus porcellus.*
3.   do.   do, larva.

METOPSILUS PORCELLUS SOCK

Shown in: Chubbie by Vice in the color Lauren. Made in size Medium with about 350 yards of yarn.
Gauge and sizing: 8 stitches in 1 inch in stockinette. Fits a foot or leg of about 7.5 [8.5, 9.5] inches.

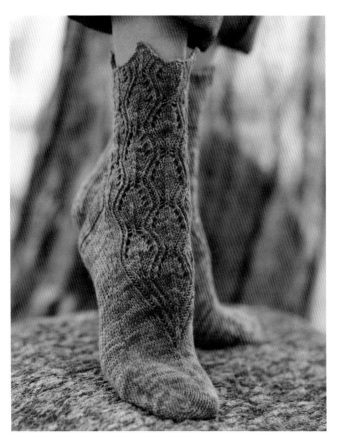

Cast on: Cast on 56 [64, 72] stitches. Place marker and join for working in the round.

Cuff and leg: Work the appropriate Main Chart until sock reaches desired height. Stop after completing row 12 [16, 20] of the Main Chart.

Heel flap: The heel flap is worked over stitches 30-56 [34-64, 38-72]. It uses 27 [31, 35] stitches.

Row 1 is a wrong-side row (worked with the inside of the sock facing you, following the wrong-side notations in the stitch key, and reading the chart from left to right). Row 2 is a right-side row (worked with the outside of the sock facing you, following the right-side notations in the stitch key, and reading the chart from right to left). Work the Heel Chart 14 [16, 18] times or until heel flap reaches desired length.

Heel turn: Odd rows are wrong-side rows (worked with the inside of the sock facing you). Even rows are right-side rows (worked with the outside of the sock facing you). Turn at the end of each row.

Row 1 (WS): Sl1, p15 [17, 19], p2tog, p1.
Row 2 (RS): Sl1, k6, ssk, k1.
Row 3 (WS): Sl1, p7, p2tog, p1.
Row 4 (RS): Sl1, k8, ssk, k1.
Row 5 (WS): Sl1, p9, p2tog, p1.

Row 6 (RS): Sl1, k10, ssk, k1.
Row 7 (WS): Sl1, p11, p2tog, p1.
Row 8 (RS): Sl1, k12, ssk, k1.
Row 9 (WS): Sl1, p13, p2tog, p1.
Row 10 (RS): Sl1, k14, ssk, k1.

For Medium and Large, as above plus:
Row 11 (WS): Sl1, p15, p2tog, p1.
Row 12 (RS): Sl1, k16, ssk, k1.

For Large, as above plus:
Row 13 (WS): Sl1, p17, p2tog, p1.
Row 14 (RS): Sl1, k18, ssk, k1.

17 [19, 21] stitches remain.

Gusset and foot:
Setup round: Pick up and knit stitches along the side of the heel flap, place first marker. Work across the top of the foot following the first row of the appropriate Foot Chart, place second marker. Pick up and knit stitches along the other side of the heel flap, k9 [10, 11]. The round now begins in the middle of the bottom of the foot.

Decrease round: K until 3 stitches remain before first marker, k2tog, k1. Work across the top of the foot following the next row of the appropriate Foot Chart. K1, ssk, k to end of round. 2 stitches decreased.

Non-decrease round: K to first marker. Work across the top of the foot following the next row of the appropriate Foot Chart. K to end of round.

Alternate decrease and non-decrease rounds until 58 [66, 74] stitches remain. Repeat the non-decrease round until you finish the appropriate Foot Chart. Repeat the last row of the appropriate Foot Chart until sock measures 2 [2.25, 2.5] inches shorter than desired length.

Toe:
Decrease round: K until 3 stitches remain before first marker, k2tog, k1. K1, ssk, k until 3 stitches remain before second marker, k2tog, k1. K1, ssk, k to end of round. 4 stitches decreased.

Non-decrease round: K to end of round.

Work these 2 rounds 4 [6, 8] times, 42 stitches remain. Work the decrease round 6 more times, 18 stitches remain. K to first marker. Remove markers. Graft toes. Weave in ends.

Stitch Key

| | RS: Knit
WS: Purl |

| ⅄ | RS: Knit through the back loop
WS: Purl through the back loop |

| — | RS: Purl
WS: Knit |

| O | Yarn over |

| → | Slip as if to purl |

| / | Right-leaning knit decrease |

| \ | Left-leaning knit decrease |

| Λ | Centered double knit decrease |

| Ⱶ | Make one right knitwise |

| Ⴘ | Make one left knitwise |

| ☐ | Repeat these stitches 3 [4, 5] times |

Heel Chart

Chart notes: The sizes use different charts. Be sure to follow the appropriate charts.

Stitches surrounded by a red border are repeated to adjust the size of the heel flap. Work them 3 [4, 5] times.

When a centered double decrease is the first stitch on the needle, it requires extra attention. The double decrease turns 3 stitches into 1. When the double decrease happens at the beginning of a needle, the first of those 3 stitches is the last stitch of the previous needle.

For example, the first stitch of round 11 of the Main Chart is a centered double decrease. The decrease will use the last stitch of round 10 and the first 2 stitches of round 11. To make the decrease, do not work the last stitch of round 10. Instead, use it as the first of the 3 stitches of the decrease as described in the stitch key. The completed stitch will be the first stitch of round 11.

Medium Main Chart

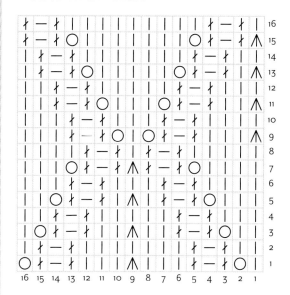

Small Main Chart

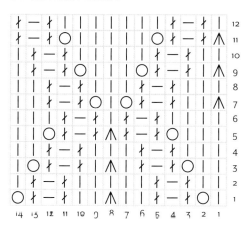

Large Main Chart

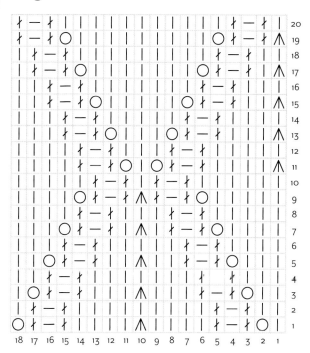

Small Foot Chart

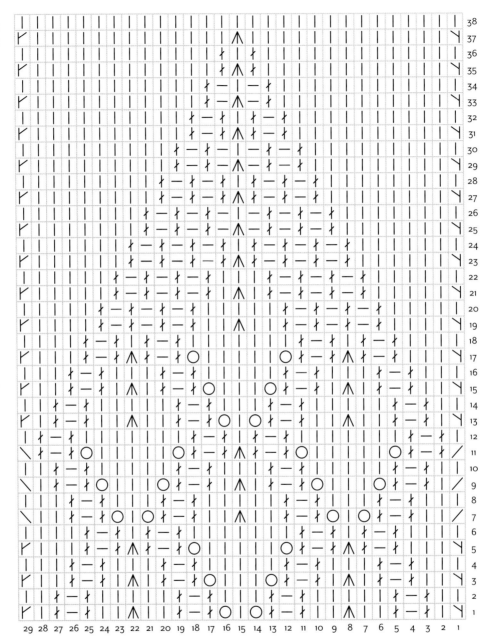

Medium Foot Chart 1

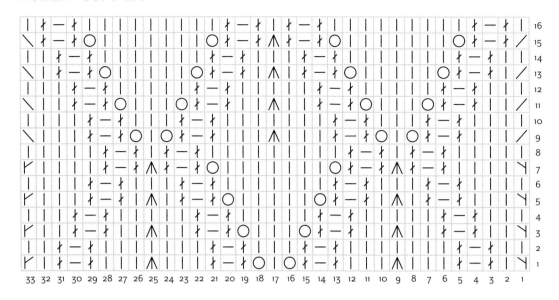

Chart notes: The Medium Foot Chart and Large Foot Chart are too big to fit easily onto one page. They have been broken across two pages. Be sure to work both parts of the chart

Medium Foot Chart 2

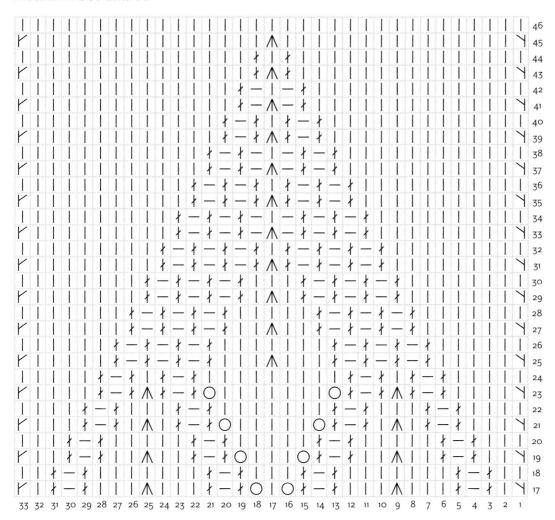

Large Foot Chart 1

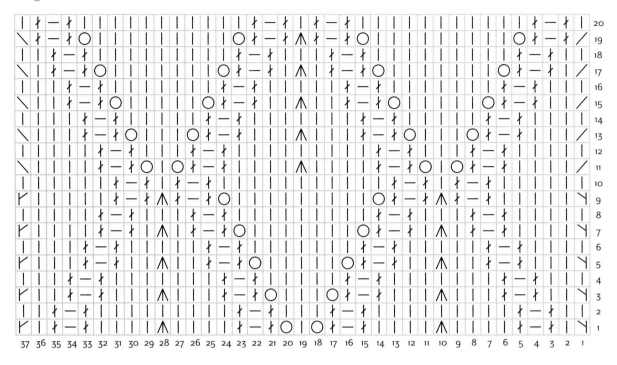

Chart notes: The Medium Foot Chart and Large Foot Chart are too big to fit easily onto one page. They have been broken across two pages. Be sure to work both parts of the chart

Large Foot Chart 2

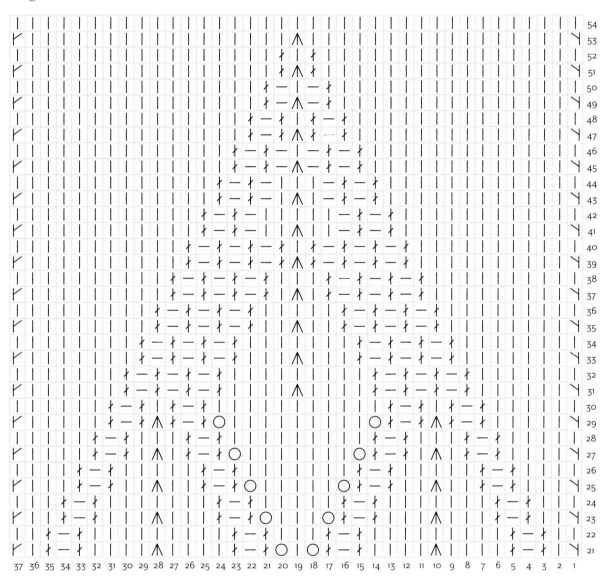

METOPSILUS PORCELLUS COWL

Shown in: Liquid Sliver by Vice in the color Stacy. Made in size Medium with about 230 yards of yarn.

Gauge and sizing: 15 stitches in 3.5 inches in Main Chart pattern (fabric expands dramatically with blocking, be sure to measure gauge over a blocked swatch). Finished circumference of 21 [31.5, 42, 52.5] inches. Height is adjustable, shown here at 9 inches.

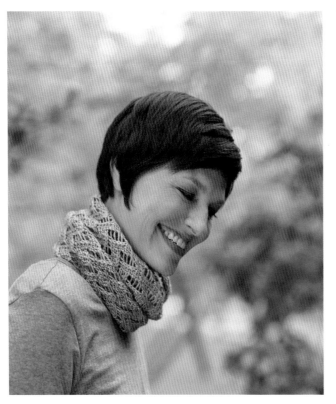

Cast on: Cast on 90 [135, 180, 225] stitches. Place marker and join for working in the round.

Body: Work the Main Chart until cowl reaches desired height (shown here worked 9 times). Stop after completing row 4 or 8 of the Main Chart.

Finishing: Remove marker. Bind off loosely. Weave in ends. Block vigorously.

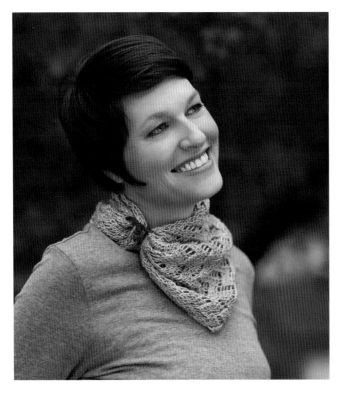

Stitch Key

| Knit

 O Yarn over

∠ Right-leaning purl decrease

∖ Left-leaning purl decrease

Main Chart

```
∠ O | | |     8
  ∠ O | | |   7
  | ∠ O | |   6
  | | ∠ O |   5
  | | | O ∖   4
  | | O ∖ |   3
  | O ∖ | |   2
  O ∖ | | |   1
6  5  4  3  2  1
```

Chart Notes: Pay special attention to round 8. When you are ready to begin round 8, slip the first stitch of the round purlwise with the yarn held to the back. Do not work the stitch, just move it to the right needle. Finish the round as shown in the Main Chart. The stitch you slipped will be worked as part of the final right-leaning purl decrease. When the round is finished, slip the final stitch of round 8 back to the left needle. It is now the first stitch of round 1.

Both sides of this stitch are pretty, and both sides of it are shown in the pictures. For convenience, the primarily knit side is called the right side in the chart, but either side is fit to show the world.

SOURCES

Vanessa antiopa projects use Lorna's Laces yarns – lornaslaces.net. The socks are made with Solemate (425 yards per skein) in Magnificent Mile. The cowl is made with Lion and Lamb (205 yards per skein) in Hermosa.

Lycaena virgaureae projects use Black Bunny Fibers yarns – blackbunnyfibers.com. The socks are made with BFL Luxe Blend (430 yards per skein) in Hedgehog's Nose. The shawl is made with Devon (600 yards per skein) in Orange Marmalade.

Polyommatus argiolus projects use Malabrigo yarns – malabrigoyarn.com. The socks are made with Arroyo (335 yards per skein) in Azules. The cuffs are made with Sock (440 yards per skein) in Impressionist Sky.

Polyommatus corydon projects use String Theory yarns – stringtheoryyarn.com. The socks are made with Caper Sock (400 yards per skein) in Blue Hill. The hat is made with Blue Faced Sport (252 yards per skein) in Grove.

Delias eucharis projects use Plucky Knitter yarns – thepluckyknitter.com. The socks are made with Plucky Feet (425 yards per skein) in Sticky Toffee. The hat is made with Primo! Worsted (200 yards per skein) in Flying Monkey.

Erasmia pulchella projects use Shibui yarns – shibuiknits.com. The socks are made with Sock (191 yards per skein) in Wasabi. The hat is made with Baby Alpaca (255 yards per skein) in Flaxen.

Danima banksiae projects use Saffron Dyeworks yarns – saffrondyeworks.com. The socks are made with Pali (360 yards per skein) in Pali. The mitts are made with Mica (230 yards per skein) in Ginger Snap.

Smerinthus ocellatus projects use Barking Dog yarns – barkingdogyarns.com. The socks are made with Achilles (400 yards per skein) in Chestnuts on the Flame. The cuffs are made with Galaxy (275 yards per skein) in Japanese Cherry.

Metopsilus porcellus projects use Vice yarns – viceyarns.com. The socks are made with Chubbie (274 yards per skein) in Lauren. The cowl is made with Liquid Sliver (231 yards per skein) in Stacy.

All charts created with StitchMastery Knitting Chart Editor – stitchmastery.com.

Photos, book, and cover design by Zoë Lonergan – zoelonergan.com.